For Chelly —

May your occult
dreams be reality —

Don

OCCULT MEDICINE

Can Save Your Life:

A Modern Doctor Looks
At Unconventional Healing

C. NORMAN SHEALY, M.D.
with Arthur S. Freese

The Dial Press   1975   New York

Library of Congress Cataloging in Publication Data

Shealy, C   Norman, 1932–
    Occult medicine can save your life.

    Bibliography: p.
        1. Mental healing.   2 Medicine, Magic, mystic,
and spagiric.   I. Freese, Arthur S., joint author.
II. Title.   [DNLM: 1. Mental healing.   2. Occult-
ism.   WB880 S5390]
RZ400.S58   615'.851   75-12910
ISBN 0-8037-8816-9

Text design by B. Klein
Manufactured in the United States of America
First printing

Contents

Acknowledgments

All books are the result of effort by many individuals. I am particularly indebted to Dr. and Mrs. Elmer Green of the Research Department, The Menninger Foundation, Topeka, Kansas, who turned me on to the use of biofeedback; to Genevieve Haller and Jeffrey Furst for steering me to the Reverend Henry Rucker, who is one of the greatest personalities I've met; to Dr. Robert Leichtman for outstanding advice; to Dr. Jerome D. Frank, Professor of Psychiatry, The Johns Hopkins University School of Medicine, for his very cogent criticism; to my research associate, Sonja Schrag, for invaluable work and rework; to Kitty Althoff, my fantastically organized secretary; to my family for sparing me to make so many trips; to the many faith healers and to the numerous investigators who provided a wealth of material and inspiration for several books; to my fellow author, Arthur Freese, for his determined persistence in detailing facts; and to him and our editor, Joyce Engelson, for their superior efforts and for telling it "like it is"—i.e., *Occult is* a many-splendored thing.

C. NORMAN SHEALY, M.D.

April 1975
La Crosse, Wisconsin

Occult Medicine
Can Save Your Life

Introduction by
Arthur S. Freese:
Dr. Norman Shealy
and His New Medicine

During our last decade, a startling, exciting new wind has sprung up from out of the East. Greeted, even cheered worldwide, it can provide a healthful cleansing, wiping away the impersonal rationality and materialistic smugness, the coldly scientific objectivity of our recent era. Known, somewhat vaguely, as the Age of Reason to those who gloried in it (especially during its height in the eighteenth and nineteenth centuries, even the early part of the twentieth), it is giving way to a whole new scene. Growing numbers of people are striving to find and do their own thing, free of the shackles of the past.

The churning about of this vast new movement is rapidly modifying, even tearing up, some of the very roots of that superscientific and purely technological culture (the Space Age, if you will), which has been the dominant theme of at least the last three decades. The now-people of our changing world have only recently begun to study the significance of this strange new era with its emphasis on the altered states of consciousness available to everyone, on a heightened sense of humane values, and on love and miracles and magic instead of technology and electronics and computers. Many of these new explorers like to emphasize these changes by giving this period its own name—the Age of Aquarius.

Thus many of us who have been present at a changing of the guard—the shifting from the Age of Reason to that of the Space Age—are now at another threshold: the Age of Aquarius. This transition has been so marked and so powerful that it has even affected that most conservative and walled-off of worlds, conventional medicine. There are already inspiring new alternatives to current medical practice which seem likely to revolutionize health care, to bring hope and help to more than three quarters of those sufferers who crowd doctors' offices. And it's not just the new doctors, but some of the old as well, who are experimenting, testing, rethinking, trying daring new approaches to match the social and cultural changes of the Aquarian Age.

Perhaps this new era will bring an end to drug tragedies and put in their place more triumphs like those of the young Texas physician who treats cancer with faith healing as well as X-rays and gets far better results, he feels, than the radiation alone could possibly achieve. One of the more respected medical journals (*Medical Economics*) reports that scores of physicians are turning to faith healers for help with their "hopeless" cases and even for their own ailments. And in the spring of 1974 a physician even wrote to the editor of *The Journal of the American Medical Association* (*JAMA*) about a bizarre psychiatric disorder called Gilles de la Tourette's syndrome and asked, "Could all of these patients be seized by the devil . . . ?"

A great involvement in the occult—parapsychology and the paranormal (the so-called psi), extrasensory perception (ESP) and clairvoyance, precognition and telepathy, even psychokinesis (PK or making physical events, such as bending nails)—has swept the globe in a massive and growing movement. But—make no mistake—medicine is only following, not leading, this worldwide movement.

Our news media reflect the broad public interest in the occult. In the last couple of years there have been feature articles on various psi phenomena (a term used to include virtually all the forms in which the occult reveals itself) in publications whose vastly different audiences indicate the breadth of today's interest. Major stories have appeared in *Time, Medical World News* (a leading medical news publication), *Science News* (a highly respected science magazine), *Popular Photography, Science Digest, The Cleveland Plain Dealer, The New York Times, Newsweek, Medical Economics,* and the *National Enquirer.* Meanwhile prestigious universities are offering courses and degrees in ESP and in magical studies, astrology, and witchcraft; one even offers lectures by the head of the Nigerian Witch Doctors' Association.

Who Believes in the Occult?

More than a few people or a few cults believe in occult powers. The famous pollster Louis Harris reported on April 29, 1974, that more than 7,000,000 Americans over the age of eighteen believe that they themselves or someone very close to them has actually been "possessed by the devil." More than a third of us apparently believe that some people are occasionally possessed, in mind or body. More than half of us believe that a devil actually exists, while only a little more than a quarter deny his existence. And in the spring of 1973, some thousand people from the Seattle area were willing to travel to the Philippines for faith healing and "psychic surgery" (in which the operator uses his bare hands, needing no anesthetic and leaving no scar after the procedure). The interest in astrology was so great that a center in New York City's Grand Central Station did a landoffice business for years, supplying computer-cast horoscopes to hurrying commuters.

But it's not just the United States that's been swept along in this wave of belief. Nat Freedland, in his recent book *The Occult Explosion*, reports a private 1955 English census which found that half the people queried believed in luck, a third had seen a fortune-teller, one-sixth believed in ghosts, and one in seventeen claimed to have actually seen a ghost. At about the same time, the German Institute of Public Opinion (according to Freedland) found that nearly a third of the Germans in a country-wide sample believed that there was some tie between the stars and human fate.

Your librarians, too, can testify to this overwhelming interest in the occult, for the great bulk of the requests they receive are for books about psi phenomena. If, as commonly happens, the books on the specific interest (clairvoyance or precognition or psychics or whatever) are out on loan, then any other about the occult seems to satisfy the seekers equally well, so great is the desire for knowledge in this field. Actually there are thousands of books on this subject. Psychic healing and surgery, for example, are attracting particular attention at this time, both from the medical profession itself and from the public at large.

But let me repeat, for it's important: physicians are not leading the way—they're only being swept along by the current. Some doctors use the occult along with the medical care they provide their patients. But for a broad utilization of all the many aspects of unconventional or occult medicine (alternative medicine, if you prefer that term), we must turn to one of America's leading neurosurgeons and pain experts, a physician who has held professorships in neurosurgery at three of America's leading medical schools: Dr. Clyde Norman Shealy of La Crosse, Wisconsin.

The Problem

Human beings have been plagued and tormented by illness and pain since they first came down out of the trees and walked upright on this earth they now think they own. And since the Stone Age, some 10,000 or 20,000 years ago, people have performed surgery. The first operations seem to have been trephining (cutting one or more circles of bone from the skulls of living patients many of whom survived either because of or in spite of their treatment) but some historians believe that finger amputations were carried out even earlier. Whether trephining was done for medical reasons (to relieve the pressure of fractured skulls, to cure headaches or epilepsy, etc.) or for religious, magical or ritual purposes cannot now be determined. But since people have always blamed disease on evil spirits or a curse or some other occult influence, these operations were probably performed for a combination of medical and religious reasons. Trephining for headaches may have been done to let evil spirits out of the head.

The earliest evidence we have of human disease is in the form of a bony tumor of the leg of one of our ancestors of a half-million years or more ago. From the first, people used surgery effectively and often—not only trephining and amputation, but the setting of broken or dislocated bones, circumcision, and castration. Medicines, too, were used right from the start, in the form of herbs and magic potions. Surgery and medicine were part of religious and magical rituals, performed by priests, medicine men, witch doctors, and shamans.

It's a long leap, though, from those days to our own period with its highly sophisticated medical care. Through all these eons, only one thing has *not* changed—human terror in the face of illness, pain, and death. But it's commonly the pain that is most dreaded. "It didn't hurt much so I paid no attention to it," is a common story doctors hear from their patients.

Yet millions of Americans suffer chronic unrelenting pain, days and nights without end, without relief. The practice of medicine is predominantly the handling of pain—the bad back, the aching head or the strange haunting agony of the lost limb (the "phantom limb" which has driven its victims to suicide), the torture of the kidney stone or that most powerful and dreaded of all pain when in the last stages the wildly growing cancer cells unremittingly squeeze the very nerves themselves in one last final frenzy. Limited as doctors still are in handling so much of disease, so often helpless in the face of death, they are even more inadequate in the face of chronic pain, for *no* medical school prepares its students properly for the management of this problem.

With his broad background in both medicine and surgery, Dr. Clyde Norman Shealy is ideally trained to view the total patient, the human being who comes seeking help for whatever reason. Sensitive and gentle, he is acutely aware of the limitations of most contemporary medical help.

Norman Shealy is unique in many ways. For one thing, he almost gave up surgery when he saw the reckless abuse of psychosurgery destroying the very core of the human being—the mind and the emotions. For Dr. Shealy believes with Hippocrates, the Father of Medicine, that the physician should "be useful, or at least do no harm." And so Dr. Shealy has exchanged the tools of his specialty—the knife and the scissors and the hemostat, the cutting and often mutilating instruments—for the more intangible, effective, and far less destructive techniques of unconventional medicine, of the occult.

Dr. Shealy has steadily sought new and better ways to help patients. His first new approach was an attempt to avoid the twin dangers of surgery and drugs. Utilizing modern scientific technology along with the insights of the occult and unconventional medicine, Dr. Shealy devised and developed a simple, safe electrical device which may be used by both a person at home and a woman in childbirth, and which can control even the pain of the last stages of cancer so that its victims need no longer depend on the usual massive doses of narcotics which supply relief only at the destructive price of a confused, stupefied half-life. Dr. Shealy's device is a sophisticated electronic version of an electrical device of a half-century and more ago—two pads are applied over the pain or over the nerves supplying the area of pain and a weak current is passed through the skin, short-circuiting and relieving the pain.

Who is Dr. Shealy?

Slightly built, of average height, Dr. Shealy has already made several classic contributions to conventional medicine and surgery.

Yet he is still a young man, just past forty—old enough to have medical maturity without having become inflexible. That he's already held professorships in three of our leading medical schools attests to the major medical breakthroughs he's achieved in his field.

One of his contributions is in the world of the ultrasmall—microsurgery—in which the doctor must work in situations so delicate that a microscope is used constantly during the operation. At these enlargements, a surgeon's fine delicate instruments look like the crude tools of a giant and suture thread is the thickness of two red blood cells. Dr. Shealy introduced to the United States a new method of using microsurgery to operate on the diseased or disordered pituitary gland buried deep in the skull—but without the traditional major brain surgery or the extensive openings into the skull to provide access from the outside.

By slipping delicate instruments up under the lip and using the microscope to guide them along the base of the nose and into the skull, Dr. Shealy accomplished the operation with a minimum of damage and danger—and more than half of the many American surgeons now utilizing this technique were trained by him. From this he went on to introduce other surgical innovations and sophisticated electronic devices to control some of the worst pains known to man, while his "pain clinic" regularly and annually restores hundreds of sufferers whose lives were overwhelmed by pain. These innovations are being copied—literally—from coast to coast and border to border while Dr. Shealy himself has already been the inspiration for innumerable other physicians.

The Step Up to Unconventional Medicine

Here then is a physician—a healer in the true sense—who has utilized Space Age science and medicine—the whole range of technology—to its maximum, then moved on to explore newer methods and ideas in healing techniques, whether occult, unconventional, or simply far out.

La Crosse is midway across our country, where the mighty Mississippi River forms the western border of Wisconsin. Doctors and medical observers from here and abroad come to La Crosse to study this new unconventional and occult medicine, to ask and to learn. For word of Dr. Shealy's accomplishments has filtered out to the medical professions. These are people who plan to return home to duplicate the work being done at La Crosse or simply to learn which patients are best referred there.

But let's backtrack a bit to see how Dr. Shealy's medical beginnings and training have led to his unique expertise. Why, in short, you should listen to his strange and exciting tale of occult medicine—and what it holds for *your* future. Here is how a modest but hard-nosed, highly trained medical scientist has utilized the full power of all our current scientific tools (ultrasophisticated medical laboratory tests, brain-wave electroencephalographs) to test and confirm anything that might conceivably offer any help for those sufferers who get no relief from today's conventional medical treatments. His carefully computerized studies have proved scientifically and statistically that psychics are as accurate in diagnosis as their white-coated opponents in the medical profession.

In one sense then this book is really a tale of success, Dr. Norman Shealy's own story of occult medicine. He tells of the electronic control of pain (regarded by some experts as one of today's major medical breakthroughs), acupuncture, and biofeedback, which he uses for practical medical purposes. He reviews all of occult medicine—its successes, uses, and failures. He tells of miracles of healing—faith healing or psychic healing or spiritual healing.

To all such material, this open-minded neurosurgeon brings the most crucial question for any healing technique: he has learned to ask simply, "Does it work?"—and then base his conclusion on what actually happens, not on what he was taught should happen nor on what he hopes will happen.

The Strange World of the Neurosurgeon

Dr. Norman Shealy's academic background would hardly lead one to expect an interest in the occult. His was an impeccably conservative and conventional scientific training, coldly objective though unusually broad and thorough. For some reason which he himself can't fathom, he decided to be a neurosurgeon when he was only in high school. At Duke University he was involved in research and at its School of Medicine he got his B.S. in medicine as well as his M.D. (in 1956). While still a medical student he began his research in neurophysiology—the functioning of the nervous system.

Perhaps it was the ultimate challenge of the human brain that attracted and fascinated the young man—the mystery of the nervous system with its amazing brain and spinal cord. In fact, thousands of years of intensive probing have failed to throw much light upon the ultimate, the intimate workings of this darkest, most superb, most mysterious part of the human being, the brain. We really still don't know what consciousness is, or sleep, or dreams. We don't even really understand what general anesthetics do to the brain.

This was the complex, confused, poorly understood area on which Dr. Norman Shealy chose to concentrate as a surgeon. The very latest knowledge has only increased our awareness of its complexity. Experts now see it as perhaps being closest to a computerized ultra-sophisticated radio-TV system whose multifaceted operations are far beyond the wildest imaginings of any of our most advanced electronic engineers.

In entering neurosurgery, Shealy accepted a particularly frustrating challenge. About half a century ago, it occurred to neurosurgeons that they need only cut the nerve pathways that pain follows up the spinal cord to the brain and they could eliminate the most severe pains. But man's nervous system has outwitted the most skilled operators, scalpel and cautery: cutting pain-conducting nerves stops pain—but only for three to six months and in not quite three-quarters of the sufferers. But how can this pain recur when the destroyed nerves don't regenerate? We actually haven't the foggiest notion, although some observers speculate that other nerves may take up the task of carrying the pain signals. In any case, an old surgical adage has described it—*you can't cut out pain with a knife.*

With the failure of this technique, the neurosurgeons moved on to attack the brain itself in an effort to stop pain—blasting that organ with ice picks and scalpels, with electrocauteries. They just plain cooked some sections. While some of these overkill measures have succeeded to a greater or lesser degree, the price has been a terrible one, for assaults on the brain (called lobotomies or psychosurgery) have altered or destroyed the very personality of the patient. But Norman Shealy remained drawn to this field, in spite of himself. He redoubled his efforts to devise nonmutilating techniques of pain relief and he became even more receptive to the gentle, nondestructive techniques of occult medicine.

Shealy's Path to the Occult

It took a long and arduous apprenticeship to join the occult to medicine. In medical school, Norman Shealy spent his summers on research in neurophysiology, the most scientifically precise and sophisticated of all medical research, demanding a knowledge of advanced electronics and computerization. He discovered things not previously known about the cerebellum, the second largest part of the brain and the coordinator of muscular movements (without the cerebellum you couldn't write smoothly or kick a football, for instance).

To round out his competence, Shealy took a medical internship and then a general surgical residency. Neurosurgery continued to attract him and he turned to Boston's famed Massachusetts General Hospital (chief hospital for the Harvard Medical School) for his neurosurgical training and spent eight months in Australia under Sir John Eccles, the 1963 Nobel Prize winner.

Shealy moved on to Cleveland's Case Western Reserve University with his first professorship in neurosurgery. Here he began his own career in earnest when he conceived the idea of putting electrodes on the spinal cord itself to short-circuit otherwise uncontrollable pain. This was certainly unconventional medicine in 1965.

The young neurosurgeon prepared the way to implement his idea with the thorough animal experimentation he'd been trained in as a scientist. He conceived his electronic device and built one. Cutting a hole the size of a quarter into the spine, he slipped the electrodes in, to lie over the pain pathways of the spinal cord itself. He called the device a "dorsal column stimulator" (DCS) for the dorsal column is that part of the spinal cord in which the pain-suppressing signals are thought to be carried up to the brain. An outside transmitter beams power to a receiver under the skin (Dr. Shealy himself describes more details later in the book) and the patient can actually dial the current necessary to stop his own pain.

First used in April 1967 on a cancer patient, the DCS worked. But Dr. Shealy is essentially conservative and he moved slowly. By 1969 he'd implanted only half a dozen of his devices. Today thousands have been placed by surgeons all over the country and the success rate in carefully selected patients can run as high as 85 percent. Here are two typical instances: a middle-aged man confined to bed by his unbearable pain following unsuccessful spinal disc surgery was freed by the DCS to lead a normally active life with his pain entirely under control. A Southern housewife had ruptured spinal discs on an African trip; unsuccessful surgery (and lack of success is common in this operation) was performed five times, leaving her confined to bed, too drugged with medication even to read properly. With Dr. Shealy's DCS she could once more lead a normal life although she still feels some pain. As she put it to me, talking of her DCS: "Bless its little heart!"

Most successful in these "spinal disc flunkouts," as Dr. Shealy terms those whose disc operations have failed, his DCS is also effective for phantom limb pain and that of nerve injuries. As Dr. Shealy has moved deeper into the occult in medicine, he has

tried to avoid even the DCS because this too involves an operation, although not the destructive one that is performed in typical
disc surgery. He feels that surgery should be avoided if possible—
and he himself does very few operations any more.

But out of this original DCS came another electronic device,
a simpler one which is much more exciting and satisfying to the
surgeon. This new one can be used by the patient himself, simply
placing it on his skin over the nerve involved, as his doctor can
show him. In this way satisfactory relief from almost all types of
pain is possible—though the degree varies. For acute pain—an injury from a fall or even the kick of a horse (as happened to Dr.
Shealy's own wife)—eight out of ten problems can be fully controlled. A Southern professor of neurosurgery has obtained relief in
some three-quarters of the patients treated with it, while an East
Coast neurosurgeon has so successfully stopped the pain of a
cancer patient that he was then able to give up completely the use
of all narcotics; previously he'd needed drugs every four hours,
around the clock. A La Crosse obstetrician has found the device
useful in childbirth, too; simply placing the electrodes on the
woman's back during the early stages of labor has proved very effective in relieving pain right up to the actual delivery.

As Dr. Shealy Sees It

Dr. Shealy's concern is not with the infection that yields so readily
to our powerful antibiotics, or the intensive-care units which save
so many lives formerly lost to heart attacks, or the necessary
surgery which has reduced the death rate of appendicitis to the
vanishing point, or the X-rays or surgery which offer so much to so
many cancer patients. For these problems, conventional medicine
is the answer and your conventional doctor the one to rely upon.
But there is a wide range of problems in that gray area of inadequate medical care where 60 or 70 or even 80 percent of the
unhappy sufferers who wander through doctors' offices cannot find

help or relief and may be turned into narcotics addicts or suffer unnecessary and mutilating surgery.

It is in this gray area that Dr. Shealy sees the role of the faith healers and the psychics, the electronic and scientific magic of biofeedback and autogenic training, or acupuncture and astrology—as well as more readily available pain clinics. Most exciting of all is Dr. Shealy's concept, his dream, of a holistic healing center where every possible modality that has been successful anywhere will be available: a sort of supermarket of medical care where the ill can sample every possible healing technique (under careful medical supervision) which has proven successful with others.

Deeply scientific, even skeptical, determined to find whatever works and make it available to all, Dr. Norman Shealy sees the future pattern of medical care at last emerging. First you would—*and should*—see your conventional doctor to get the best he or she has to offer. Then, for those not helped by orthodox treatment, there would be the new holistic healing center with its varieties of occult and unconventional medicine.

What This Book Is All About

This book is really Dr. Shealy's own story of what he himself has seen or has proved of the successes and values of the occult, or unconventional, or nontraditional, or alternative medicine which he is pioneering. But just a word on what is really meant by occult: it means hidden or concealed, whether information or hard-to-see blood in the body's wastes or products—something known only to a special few. But the exact meaning I'll leave to Dr. Shealy's explanation later on, for this use of "occult" is rightly his.

In any case, our world already has occult help available for those health problems which are still beyond the limited capabilities of today's conventional therapies. But in this book you also find some new suggestions—startling perhaps but with scientific evidence—for a future approach to the delivery of health care, a proposal, and a plea for a new medical therapy—one administered with love. And perhaps it is this love that is really lacking in today's medical practice.

As Dr. Norman Shealy puts it: "There is a magic in medicine, there always has been—and this is why medical miracles are a recognized and well-documented aspect of professional practice and medical care. Perhaps that magic is love-energy, perhaps it's faith—for certainly no patient has ever been helped or cured or healed unless he has had faith in what his doctor is doing for him.

"In any case, the doctor's task today is to put that magic—that faith—back into medicine where it belongs, to learn to make the miracles available for the patient when nothing else can help!"

Dr. Norman Shealy begins his own story with what is best known as "faith healing"—where the dead are restored to life and "miraculous" cures performed. Here you will find the attempts at scientific explanation of these occurences—there is nothing so awesome as the restoration to life of a human being seemingly dead, or the healing of a stricken sufferer. Then, you will learn the rest of the story: how Dr. Shealy himself came to occult medicine, the many ways occult medicine *can* save your life, what occult medicine is accomplishing today, and what this whole new world of health care promises for the future.

Faith Healing, the Occult, and Me

1

Faith Healing and Medicine

This is a book about *you*—your life and your health and, most of all, your healing when you are ill. In the four million years or so that humanity and its forebears are now believed to have wandered about on this globe, we have consistently turned to faith healing by shaman and medicine man, by Great Mother and priest, and the witch doctor has imperceptibly faded into today's doctor. The strange paint and bizarre clothing of the ancient witch doctor have turned into the white coat and the hospital-green mask and cap and operating gown plus rubber gloves, leaving only a tiny bit of skin and eyes visible (not so very different from the animal skins or feathers or paint of primitive people).

In a very real sense, medicine is now—as it always has been—faith healing. Without the patient's faith in his physician and his treatment there can be no hope for cure. Surgeons have long known—we have all known—that the will to live, and faith in the healer and the healing, are essential to recovery. They are primary factors without which there is no hope.

So there really should be no surprise at the "miracles" of Lourdes or the classic laying-on-of-hands that produces cures in patients given up for lost by conventional medicine. In fact, there may be no magic here at all—only the power of the mind, the psyche, over the body processes. For faith healing—whether of conventional medicine or occult medicine (which I like to call simply unconventional medicine)—may work its so-called "magic" by producing changes in the autonomic nervous system, that part of you which keeps your body operating automatically. It sees to it that your heart beats properly, that you breathe enough to supply sufficient oxygen for brain and body, that your stomach and intestines digest and pass along the food you eat, that your kidneys keep on filtering your blood, and so on.

So it seems only logical that my first chapter should be devoted to the healing part of occult medicine—what we call "faith healing." As in the rest of this book, you will find both faces of the coin here—the good and the bad, the useless along with practical facts or thoughts you can use to get help for yourself.

A Houston police captain stood in the front of a huge jam-packed Los Angeles auditorium literally to be knocked to the floor by the gentlest touch of a woman healer's hands—and be cured of an "incurable cancer." A Northeastern man in his sixties lay dying of a fatal heart attack in a Boston hospital—to be healed by his young minister's prayers. A New Englander, equally seriously stricken, was roused from a three-week coma by the same kind of prayers—only to die an hour or so later (and yet this too was a healing!). And across the seas at famed Lourdes, innumerable sufferers have gained help and nearly a hundred have been entirely cured of their fatal or near-fatal illnesses. Healings at Lourdes must meet such rigorous and demanding criteria that many more known cures would surely be included if the standards were merely the usual critical ones of scientific accuracy.

All healings are miracles in a very human sense. The occurrence of a healing of any kind invariably leaves the participants, even those who only witness it, with a deep sense of awe at what they have suddenly, somehow, found themselves a part of. The unique and very special nature of all healings—their mysterious and almost other-worldly character—is present whether they are performed by masked and gowned doctors carrying out their amazing medical rites in the coldly gleaming scientific healing temples we call hospitals; by the strange rites of painted and half-naked witch doctors in the depths of distant regions where the natives still live in a primitive yesterday; or even by the simple laying-on-of-hands in the heart of the financial district of modern materialistic New York City.

Yet, despite the seeming disparity among these healings, there is a common thread, running through them all. For these could only come about through the power of faith and love (in the broadest, most all-encompassing sense)—and perhaps these two— faith and love—are really the same. Originally I came to this conclusion through my own clinical observations, buttressed by a good deal of hard thinking and consideration; but now independent, solid scientific data have been found to confirm it.

Long experience has taught physicians that a patient's faith in his doctor is essential if his medical problem is to be helped. Much of this faith grows out of the patient's recognition of his doctor's empathy or love—when the sick person feels that his physician really cares about him as a human being, not just another case. Also the wise, compassionate physician doesn't try to tear down a patient's beliefs in an honest sincere nonmedical healer— he will be more concerned with his patient's well-being than his own desire to be the only healer around. Tearing down a patient's faith to preserve a doctor's status is all too common in the medical profession—and a tragically destructive way to practice medicine.

Like every experienced surgeon, I can tell you that any patient who is over-fearful or unusually depressed, who expects the worst, who has no faith in an operation's chance of success, will surely have the poorest possible chance of survival. The patient who enters surgery with confidence in the result, with faith in his surgeon's ability, sincerity and desire to help, with strong expectations of recovery, always stands the best chance. And experienced medical practitioners, too, can tell you that the patient with no faith in his medication or treatment actually stands little chance of being healed.

These facts have always been related as anecdotes—one doctor after another telling his or her experiences. Now there is scientific proof that doctors' observations and common folk knowledge are statistically factual. For instance, a recent study has shown that one of the major factors influencing the success of the eyesight-saving surgery for retinal detachment is (in the words of the team headed by Dr. Randall C. Mason of Chicago) ". . . a high degree of confidence that the surgery will be successful. . . ."

A careful study by Dr. Jerome D. Frank, professor of psychiatry at The Johns Hopkins University, revealed that the recovery of American soliders from *schistosomiasis*, a parasitic blood infestation, was dependent on the men's emotional condition; those who failed to recover were found to feel unloved and to have lost their faith in their doctors. Even full recovery from Asian flu, as has been clearly shown by a Johns Hopkins medical team, depends on the emotional state of the patient, something which the doctor— the healer—can handle only by providing the love and faith these soldiers with *schistosomiasis* lacked.

Healing is clearly a multifaceted affair and, tragically, the rigid adherents of conventional medicine ignore what recent research into psychotherapy has shown to be the most vital element in healing—the personality of the therapist. The elements of personality most important for healing success are empathy and warmth, sincerity or honesty—and the ability to enhance a positive expectancy on the part of the patient. Studies have even shown that the chances for improvement in psychotherapy are almost doubled when the therapist possesses faith and love and sincerity in abundance. It's also been shown that these qualities are the responsibility of the healer (in this case the psychotherapist), because the patient's characteristics don't influence the outcome— something doctors don't like to admit. They would prefer to blame the patient. And it's my opinion that these qualities of love and sincerity explain the consistent success of certain of the faith healers.

A healer's love and sincerity can even improve the academic performance of college students undergoing therapy. Children learn to read faster when their teachers have these qualities. In fact, every really good faith healer that my associate and I have known (and we've known a good proportion of our country's outstanding ones as well as some from abroad) has exhibited love and sincerity. When there's trust and faith, when the physician or healer is loving and concerned, when the sufferer's expectation of help is great—then the most amazing things can and do happen.

A physician, some seven or eight years ago, learned he had a particularly deadly tumor for which immediate amputation of a limb was recommended. But this is a terrible price even for life itself. (I know a young college instructor who refused to have a leg amputated, preferring to die instead.) The physician started praying and one day stumbled on a book written by the great healer Olga Worrall and her husband. The physician started attending the Worralls' healing services. Meanwhile his doctor continued to check the tumor. This type of tumor commonly grows and spreads until fatal—but something strange was happening. Instead of succumbing to the cancer, the physician recovered. The tumor disappeared. His doctor was astounded but the patient-physician took it in stride, for he had been *sure* he was going to recover.

Working for this physician were all the elements that I feel go into the miracle of faith healing: the faith and belief of the sick person; the warmth and love and sincerity of the healer; the patient's positive expectations of cure. I personally suspect—although there's no proof of this yet—that some physiological changes do take place in faith healing; perhaps there are autonomic nervous system involvements and modifications of some endocrine or nerve functioning, perhaps some changes at the deepest levels of the human brain which go back to a prehuman level. But whatever it is that happens, it does happen and it does heal—of that I'm sure.

The placebo is one of our most powerful drugs (certainly it's our safest). It was virtually the only drug we had until quinine was recognized as a relief for malaria little more than 300 years ago. You've heard of placebos as "sugar pills," and commonly they are just that—lactose or milk sugar. Today's conventional doctors tend to sneer at placebos as pharmacologically inert (having no physical or chemical effect on the body)—and succeed only in revealing their own lack of understanding of medicine and patient care. For these same doctors are the ones who also sneer at the bedside manner, and we've seen it proved that without the love and commitment which some call "bedside manner," no doctor can hope to heal successfully or consistently.

But the whole thing is much bigger than just "sugar pills." For what we're really talking about here is not a pill but the so-called "placebo effect"—a general psychological or psychosomatic effect, as opposed to a physical effect. *Any* therapy that produces an emotional effect is regarded by some as a placebo. Thus the ancient Royal Touch (the laying-on-of-hands) has been regarded by many observers as a "placebo." Many of today's conventional doctors have sacrificed a powerful tool by ignoring the placebo.

When hypodermic syringes first came into use a little over a hundred years ago a French physician discovered that water injections were as effective as morphine injections in the control of one patient's pain. Excited by what he thought was a great discovery, he reported this and for many years thereafter the medical journals carried articles telling of the wonders of water injections for the control of severe pain. But once the newness of the injection technique wore off, water placebos lost their potency and relieved pain about the same as any other placebo—for sugar pills *do* relieve pain in nearly one-third of patients, across the board. Take a large enough sample of even patients with terminal cancer, and placebos will control pain in about 30 percent. Add strong suggestions to the situation and the percentage jumps to about fifty.

But this can work in the opposite way too—for drugs are tricky and much depends on the way the doctor or healer gives them. If the physician believes the placebo will really work—if he has faith in it and gives it with love-energy—it can help as many as 80 percent of his patients; a negative attitude can reduce the effectiveness as much as 70 percent.

Suggestion can also reverse the action on nonplacebos. Syrup of ipecac, which is used widely to induce vomiting, can prevent nausea and vomiting in pregnant women if given with the strong suggestion that the drug will stop the nausea. Similarly, if you give placebos to patients who have no faith in you, you're likely to get a severe negative reaction—vomiting or hives, for example.

Remember that the "placebo effect" isn't limited to sugar pills or liquids or capsules. It is involved in any therapy—"soak your hand in hot water" or "apply ice" or "we'll operate and remove the cause of the problem."

A recent heart surgery technique which has caught the fancy of the popular press should serve as a reminder to doctors that it is the placebo effect that heals—not useless drugs and life-threatening operations. In this procedure, a blood vessel from the chest wall is connected to the heart muscle to increase the supply of blood and oxygen and relieve the terrible gripping chest pains of angina pectoris. Early reports on the operation (like those on the water injections) were enthusiastic and some still are—the relief from pain made the risk acceptable. But some surgeons got suspicious. They performed a false operation, with all the panoply of the real thing—the chest incision and all—except that the blood vessel wasn't touched. The pain was relieved just as well by the mock surgery as by the real.

Clearly, as long as the patient has faith—a positive expectancy—that what is being done will relieve his pain, then the pain *will* be relieved.

It's been said there's much of the doctor in the witch doctor—and much of the witch doctor in the doctor! In fact, this is what makes both of them just a little more effective. As I see it, physician, witch doctor, shaman, medicine man are all essentially faith healers and always have been. When the modern American physician abandoned his bedside manner, the public began complaining of the loss of the old-fashioned family doctor.

The ancient witch doctor used intuitive understanding of the suffering patient to heal. The early physician used the psychological. For neither of these had enough medical or scientific knowledge to heal by the potency of their treatments. The early healers marshalled love and warmth and faith and sincerity to heighten the patient's expectancy of cure (whether by promises or drums or chants or magical dances).

But the post-World War II supertechnological age led the medical profession to embrace the concept of the "scientific" doctor: cold, distant, always holding patients at arm's length; disdaining "bedside manner," the laying-on-of-hands, the closeness, and sincerity which millions of years of human existence on this planet have proved so necessary to healing. If something is broken or malfunctioning, simply replace it or repair it with efficient superior technical know-how. Today's physician is trained in the mechanistic approach even to life itself. He comes to see the treatment of disease as simply a matter of bringing technological know-how to bear on the offending part or organ or tissue with neither concern for nor interest in the human being to whom it all belongs.

Technological medicine has freed humanity from many of its ills, and driven death back into its proper place, at the end of a full and healthy life. But the price for all this has been steep: a system of medical care most of whose practitioners repair human beings as though they were air-conditioners—simply to restore smooth operation with a minimum of personal involvement: "walk in, do your job, and leave."

As a result of this approach, increasing numbers of patients are turning to practitioners of unconventional medicine. Many of these are legitimate, honest, and successful faith healers. Others are offbeat cultists or even outright quacks. Far more patients are now being treated by alternative methods than by conventional ones, simply because traditional medicine no longer provides what the public needs and wants.

The public turns to the practitioners of occult medicine because they have one characteristic in common—they look on the patient as a total human being. They offer emotional help, love, personal warmth and involvement, sincerity, and an ability to mobilize the individual sufferer's expectations of help.

No honest objective observer can dispute the fact that faith healers do heal—but there are still those who try to disprove it by citing individual instances of "failure."

Even if it were true that faith healers cure only psychosomatic disorders (and I'll show you how much more they do), then the faith healers would be benefitting the 85 percent who enter doctors' offices and get no help there. Doctors see as many psychosomatic disorders today as did Galen (the great first-century physician of the Roman Empire) who estimated that these problems affected 60 percent of his patients. Very likely these problems haven't changed much since people first came out of the caves. In one study of more than 100 new patients entering the medical clinic of Massachusetts General Hospital, investigators found psychological disturbances in 84 percent. In another 1,000 patients referred to the diagnostic clinic at Mount Sinai Hospital in New York City, investigators found that 81.4 percent had emotional factors at the basis of their complaints while 69 percent had no physical disorder at all.

Faith healing seems miraculous because it seems to defy all our usual biological and chemical laws and rules, but it does work. But, as in all healing, you must protect yourself—and knowledge is your best weapon. Let's also look at the quackery which creeps in at times (as it does in every profession) and see how to tell the honest from the phony, while examining what the sincere healers can do.

It might be wise first to say a word about the very term "faith healer," for these people are also known as psychic healers or spiritual healers. The term used depends more on the person speaking than any sharp or widely recognized differences. Each person interested in healing tends to use the term with which he or she feels most comfortable. The terms are often used interchangeably but some do differentiate by saying that not all healers are psychics (a debatable point itself) while others decry the word "faith" on the grounds that an infant can be healed and yet can't be said to have faith. Still others like the term "spiritual healer" because they feel the healing comes about through the power of prayer, by God's power, and the healer acts only as a conduit to direct and channel this power.

My associate and I decided to use the term "faith healer" chiefly because it's the one most familiar to the greatest number of people and also likely to meet the broadest acceptance. Moreover, "faith healer" does seem preferable because it covers the widest range of practices. For example it can even include those physicians who practice the best kind of medicine—whose warmth and sincerity give their patients faith in them.

The Faith Healers:
The Legitimate and
the Quacks

I want to show what two of our healers are like as people and in detail before we cover the field in general. These two are Mrs. Olga Worrall of Baltimore, whose fame as a healer is worldwide and to whom doctors turn when they need help for themselves; and a minister of one of New York City's oldest and most prestigious churches, Reverend F. Deeply committed to his calling, Reverend F. has asked that his name be withheld so that he might not compromise his usefulness to both the ministry in general and the healing ministry in particular—for this area is still somewhat controversial. Reverend F. is concerned that the material we include here might disturb those in his church or his religious order who are still conservative and see the healing ministry in a different light, who might then feel uncomfortable about seeking his help for their spiritual needs. However, he feels so strongly about the healing ministry—as do many others in it, both here and in Great

Britain—that he still wants the facts about it presented to both those who minister (the clergy) and those who receive this ministration (the public).

Mrs. Olga Worrall is one of the best known of American healers. She's a rarity chiefly because she's accepted so widely by the conventional medical profession that scores of physicians have themselves come to her for healing when their personal ailments became too much for their own colleagues to cure. Mrs. Worrall recalls the evening when nearly a dozen physicians were in her house in quiet suburban Baltimore—all seeking healing for their own illnesses. There's a steady stream of patients sent by their physicians to seek her help—often with notes detailing the medical problem, certifying that the patient is under medical care and asking for anything the healer could provide since conventional medicine had run out of possibilities.

Only recently, Mrs. Worrall spoke on her forty years of unconventional healing at a two-day symposium held at Stanford University and attended by nearly 500 physicians and scientists. Some of the physicians brought this gifted healer ten patients who couldn't be helped by conventional medicine. Seven of these ten were either improved or cured by her healing. And in her home there are four-drawer filing cabinets bulging with the records of healings by her and her late husband. Unfortunately there is no research money available to go through these files for the long-term analyses and doublechecking needed for a truly scientific evaluation.

Olga Worrall says, "It should all be called healing. We don't call a doctor's healing 'spiritual' or 'faith' healing; we just call it healing."

Her technique is simplicity itself—the classic combination of prayer and the laying-on-of-hands. At the end of the formal church service, those seeking help come to the altar rail where the healer softly asks the problem and then places her hands on the ailing part as she prays for help.

Mrs. Worrall is a grandmotherly warm person—the last one people would be likely to identify as a clairvoyant (which she is) or a faith healer. Now in her late sixties, she lost her husband in 1972 after a long happy marriage during which they both practiced healing, for his psychic and healing gifts paralleled hers. They never accepted any money or gifts of any kind for their services. In fact, the respected medical magazine *Medical Economics* recently reported that an extensive search had not turned up a single patient who had ever been allowed to give her either gifts or money, even though many had tried to do so. Her faith-healing service is conducted on Thursday mornings at Baltimore's Mount Washington Methodist Church and not even a collection plate for the church is passed. This is the world-renowned "New Life Clinic" which Ambrose and Olga Worrall helped their minister found.

Mrs. Worrall is a frank, down-to-earth woman who calls people "Honey" and "Sweetie" and says "You're doggone right." Those who seek her aren't afraid to ask her for "another shot of healing." As she says, "We talk very unholy."

Her advice is simple, direct and sincere: "If a person is sick he should go to a good doctor and then also employ prayer or spiritual healing. . . . It's absolutely *dangerous* to advise anyone *not* to see the doctor—*you use all forms of healing!*"

Typically, this healer is both humble and honest: "I have people coming to me with tumors and all sorts of things and every once in a while we hit the jackpot. We make no promises—every healing is an experiment. We never know what's going to happen. But a very high percentage who come have been touched."

The healings have become innumerable over the years. I give only a few instances here.

One woman was to have an operation for uterine cysts and the healer's hands on her abdomen felt so hot they burned. The day after her second visit to the Worralls, the woman was turned away from the hospital—the doctor cancelled the operation because he couldn't find the tumor anymore.

A college girl from the South developed a lump in her breast and wrote a letter asking Olga Worrall to pray for her. The healer suggested that the young woman join her in prayer every night at nine o'clock for five minutes, "turning your thoughts toward God and visualizing that energy which builds and rebuilds, pouring into your body," but insisted as always that the young woman see her doctor at the same time. The next letter told that within a week the lump had disappeared and she was able to graduate with high honors.

Another woman, who had a severe blood disorder, was referred to Olga Worrall by her doctor. She had been given only one month to live. Within six months, the doctor reported, "We don't know what's happened but the whole blood picture has changed— it's back to normal." That was fourteen years ago and the woman is still alive.

The wife of a professional man called because her husband's physicians had ordered an exploratory operation for appendicitis. The healer recalls saying, "He doesn't have appendicitis—his gall bladder is loaded with stones." X-rays had shown no stones. The healer, who knows nothing about X-rays ("I'm only a housewife," she says) gave directions for taking new X-rays. She still has the telegram that followed: "You've hit the jackpot—gall bladder has over 100 stones . . . was loaded when they opened it up . . . appendix all right."

This is healing in the broadest, most valuable sense. Olga Worrall feels she is tapping an energy source—the power of prayer, of God.

And in New York City is a famous old church whose minister, the Reverend F., has been in the healing ministry for some fifteen years, since he was first trained (along with lay people and psychiatrists) by Agnes Sanford, another of America's great faith healers. The Reverend still speaks of the psychiatrist who told of having been cured by Agnes Sanford of an "incurable" disease: "For a clergyman to hear a psychiatrist say this is something. Because it happened, it strengthens your faith."

Reverend F. recalls: "Fifteen years ago when I began [the healing ministry], people really did think you were nuts . . . except for the doctors, and that's interesting for they were much more open than the clergy, would say frankly, 'We're mechanics, put a body together the best we can and hope like hell it mends.

We don't heal anybody—it's Mother Nature or the mystery of the Universe or something. . . .' "

Reverend F. explains, "I'm fairly pragmatic. I'm not intuitive and I'm not a mystic. I came into this whole ministry with difficulty. There's something in the human soul which responds to this kind of prayer. I don't understand it and that's why I think it's important for people who are scientifically inclined to look at this. I figure if you get sick you hit all bases: you go to a doctor with your body, you go to a psychiatrist with your mind, you go to a clergyman with your spirit—and you do all three simultaneously because you're not split up into three sections, you're a whole person."

Reverend F. also uses the laying-on-of-hands at the altar rail. He's been involved, like almost all serious healers, in cancer problems and reports that there have occasionally been spontaneous remissions following prayer. "When you pray, you're always praying for a spontaneous remission."

He regards three instances as typifying his whole ministry of healing:

He himself experienced the first healing. He'd developed enormous warts covering the entire back of one hand. It was about noontime and he was praying for a woman at the rail when he felt something happening (an intuitive awareness he's become accustomed to when a healing really takes place—"a sense of presence"). About two in the afternoon he looked at the warts and they were actually disappearing. By the time he went home at four they were gone. He asked his wife, "Am I crazy?" As he says, smiling, "I believe, but I still have doubts."

The next case was more serious. Following his first healing conference, he came back "all revved up—which is what happens." One of the men of his church had been in a coma since a heart attack three weeks earlier: "I went barging into his room and threw the nurse out. I was going to prove it all." Reverend F. put his hands on the man's head and prayed. The man opened his eyes and spoke for the first time: "Do it again." The minister did and the same thing happened—three times in all. He left the hospital convinced the man was healed—but he died within an hour. The Reverend had to live with that until he concluded that the man had been unable psychically to die. Death was *his* healing; only after he'd been healed was he finally able to die peacefully.

The third case was a man in his sixties in a Northeastern state who had just been taken to the hospital with cardiac arrest (heart stoppage). On the way into the emergency room, the doctor shook his head at Reverend F. and said the man was gone. Everything had been done—defibrillation, drugs, everything—and everything had failed. He couldn't last more than four or five minutes. The minister went in and prayed. He left convinced the patient was going to die. But the patient was out of the hospital in two weeks, fully recovered and now, eight years later, he's still racing around the countryside (for he's an extremely active person). Later, the minister worked up his courage and asked the doctor what had happened. The doctor said, "He was dead as far as I was concerned. I just don't know any way to explain it." The minister sums it all up: "I tell you these things because to me they really encompass the healing ministry. They've made me realize we're not dealing with magic and we're not dealing with some kind of placebo—we're dealing with the realities of life and death, and the healing ministry has to be put into that context."

We use these two healers as examples because by far the greatest number of legitimate faith healers feel their healing power comes from either prayer or God. Another, much smaller, group feels they're tapping some universal or personal source of energy while a third small group talks of the spirit world which does the healing. The one near-universal belief among healers is that healing comes from the power of love—the love of God or a universal love-energy or just love itself.

Looking at a few more instances of healing may help to clarify the process somewhat.

Kathryn Kuhlman is the famous Pittsburgh healer who treated the Houston police captain mentioned earlier. You can find his story in her latest book, *Nothing Is Impossible with God*.

In this same book is the story of a professor of medicine at

The Johns Hopkins University and his wife. Their daughter was born with a dislocated hip and her doctor spoke of surgery, braces, even a body cast—and the possibility of a permanent limp or worse. The young parents had already fulfilled Kathryn Kuhlman's advice of doing everything medically possible and then turning to faith, to God. After a simple prayer of their own, they took the little girl, now several months old, to one of Miss Kuhlman's healing services in Pittsburgh where they then lived. As the young father watched, the little leg began to straighten, slowly moving into normal position. They kept their appointment with their orthopedic surgeon, who looked and poked and tested. There was nothing wrong. The child was perfectly normal. The referring doctor was amazed and could only attribute the change to God.

Healers in general seem to feel that most or all of us can heal to some degree; it's mainly a matter of putting to use faculties ordinarily dormant.

Dr. Lawrence LeShan, widely known parapsychologist and experimental psychologist, has devised a training seminar which turns the majority of those attending into healers in the course of a five-day but terribly exhausting schedule. It took Dr. LeShan years of observation and long study of successful healers such as the Worralls, Agnes Sanford, and Kathryn Kuhlman—along with difficult and demanding experimentation—to develop the method of healing which he teaches at these seminars. He tells of a seventy-five-year-old woman (in his recent book, *The Medium, the Mystic, and the Physicist*) whose painful arthritis kept her from touching her fingers to her palm. It took this healer fifteen minutes, part of it with her hand between his, to enable this woman to close her hand fully and without pain.

And there is the great wonder of Lourdes, France. Almost 3,000,000 pilgrims visit Lourdes annually and almost 50,000 of these are sick or disabled. The pilgrimage is an exciting one, exhilirating and uplifting; the expectations are intense. As has been said, this trip is never made in vain—for the emotional uplift it gives is enormous. Those who try to prove scientifically that some healings are not perfect cures either fail to recognize or prefer to ignore the reality that neither faith healing nor conventional medicine can achieve perfect results. Even though an ideal cure may not be achieved, a more satisfying and functional life is a success too.

At Lourdes is the ultimate proof that physical disease can be cured by faith healing. The numbers reported by the Roman Catholic Church are clearly understated and too low.

Quackery is a problem that haunts all legitimate people in the whole area of the occult—faith healers, psychics, interested physicians—because suspicion and skepticism of the field are deeply embedded in the public mind. Honest professionals in the field (and most *are* honest) are even more disgusted and angered than the public at large by any quackery.

When recently the news media carried seemingly well-proven attacks on the Philippine psychic surgery as fraudulent, the occult world wasn't badly hurt because this has always been a fringe activity. But when the media reported that the young director of Dr. J. B. Rhine's famous Institute for Parapsychology at Duke University had been faking research data in PK experiments with mice, it was a disturbing setback for a field which has attained considerable respect as a scientific pursuit. However, only four months earlier the chief of an important laboratory at New York's prestigious Sloan-Kettering Institute for Cancer Research was investigated for faking research results on mice. In both instances, it was scientific colleagues in the same field who called a halt. I think both cases are simply a matter of the failings of an individual.

One of Olga Worrall's stories exemplifies a more obvious problem. When her late minister, Dr. Day (who founded the New Life Clinic), was out in California early in the century, the maid of a minister friend practically pulled the dishes away from the dinner guests because she had to attend a meeting. For some reason, Dr. Day followed her and found her going to a famous evangelist's meeting. When those who wanted to be saved were told to come forth, the healthy maid suddenly hobbled down the aisle on a pair of crutches, was touched by the evangelist and then—dramatically throwing away her crutches—went running up the aisle crying, "I'm healed—I'm saved!" When Dr. Day questioned her about it later she was frank: "I get five dollars for that—more than I get for being a maid."

But the maid isn't the only one, for the well-known psychic observer Susy Smith tells of a New York City woman who does the same thing—only she retrieves her crutches each time to have them ready for the next visiting evangelist. As Susy Smith sums it up in her book, *How to Develop Your ESP:* "That woman's in show biz!"

Olga Worrall after all these years still feels shocked at such stories. "I call that dirty pool and this is once where I think horsewhipping wouldn't be too harsh. It really shook me up when I heard of it."

But how can *you* protect yourself if you want an honest healer? As yet, you can't look up a healer's credentials as you can a doctor's. But you can find knowledgeable people to vouch for the healer. You might start by asking your minister or even your doctor if they know something about a particular healer or if they can recommend one. If they are prejudiced or ignorant about this field, you could then ask your minister or regional church organization to put you in touch with one of two relatively new and still not too well-known organizations which are particularly interested in faith healing and could certainly refer you to a legitimate faith healer: the Order of St. Luke (42 Myrtle Avenue, Irvington, New Jersey 07111) and the Schools of Pastoral Care (a list of which can be obtained from Spiritual Frontiers Fellowship, 800 Custer Avenue, Evanston, Illinois 60202).

One of the major advantages of the eventual acceptance by the medical profession of the validity of occult medicine will be that the patient can get a referral from his physician to a legitimate faith healer, just as he now gets one to a medical specialist in any other field.

Reverend F. made a helpful point in discussing quackery in occult medicine: "The only thing I would say was wrong in going to a quack would be if he should tell you not to follow your doctor's advice—heck, anybody can pray with me and prayer can help. But if this person told me not to make use of the medical resources that are available then I would be worried." I want to underscore his point. Any nonphysician who tells you to forget your doctor's advice is a quack.

Mrs. Worrall, Reverend F., and I all say see your doctor, follow his or her advice, and seek that extra something which faith healers have to offer. In short, use every conventional and unconventional healing technique that today's world has to offer. I think this is the best advice.

We have seen that healers can save lives given up for lost. We have seen these healings cover the whole range of medical practice from the minor wart to deadly heart attacks and cancer. There is almost no condition that faith healing cannot help even though it may only be an extra something added to the basic medical care. The broken bone has to be set, the cancer or the appendix may have to be removed—but the success with conventional treatment may be higher and convalescence quicker and easier. If you're a diabetic and have to take insulin, you must continue it but I've known of doctors who were able to reduce the daily amount needed when the patient had faith healing. *However, the doctor must be the judge of that.*

In short, faith healing can give an added dimension of help in any medical situation where a doctor monitors the condition, ready to intervene if the faith healing should fail (and it does on occasion—like any other form of medical treatment).

What I want to see is further medical and scientific investigation to lay down careful guidelines for the use of this amazing medical tool whose use seems so simple, safe, and comfortable.

What is the process of faith healing like? Olga Worrall, after almost half a century of healing and seeing other healers, says, "Each one is a law unto himself and no two people work alike in this field."

Many, like Reverend F., simply place their hands on the person's head (the classical laying-on-of-hands) and say a prayer while others like Olga Worrall place their hands on the troubled part. Henry Rucker, a Chicago psychic and healer, may wave his hand across the room or pass his hands over the body without touching it; Dr. LeShan may position his hands around the affected part or just concentrate psychically on the healing. Some healers do dramatic things such as waving their hands or pointing their fingers, making the "taking-away" pass followed by the "throwing-away" pass (gesturing as if grabbing something with their hand and then throwing it on the ground or off into the distance).

Then there is absent healing, often done over considerable distances. Someone calls or writes for help. Commonly the sufferer is told to "tune in" or pray at a certain time when the healer will also be praying. It does work for Olga Worrall and Henry Rucker (who will be discussed later). Harry Edwards, the great English healer, has also done a good deal of absent healing.

How does it feel? The healers themselves commonly find that their hands feel hot or warm. Olga Worrall has felt little difference in hers; they do not feel warm, but sometimes she feels a little prickly sensation. Reverend F. feels a power or energy coursing through his hands, a sensation of heat, and he can actually see his hands redden and occasionally there is even a tremor. He says, "I don't pay too much attention to it. It's not something I can turn on or off."

The healees—the patients—commonly report a feeling of heat, and many also describe a vibration "like an electrical vibrator," an electrical shock, or a tingling sensation. Some, however, simply report nothing at all. Yet the healers, despite their differences in actions or sensations do heal; and the sufferers, regardless of what they feel—or don't feel—are healed.

We just don't understand what's going on, or why people differ so much in their experiences. I speculate that whatever is happening in a healing may be different in each person, or that the heat and other sensations are just meaningless side effects which have nothing to do with whatever it is that's actually producing the healing. Only the future—and more scientific technical studies—will answer our questions.

How does faith healing work? This of course is the great question to which we have only the faintest hint of answers as yet. There's a lot of vague talk in the occult fraternity about the energy of the universe, the power out there somewhere which some think they can concentrate between their palms by their personal powers or charisma. There's talk of the power of prayer and of God, while others speak of the spirits on which they call for help.

Olga Worrall says, "We *all* have the capacity but some to a greater degree than others—it's a natural ability you inherit. It's love, and you can't heal without love." But Reverend F. sees the healing as coming from deep within the psyche so that if you can push through the barriers and get far enough down into its deepest levels you can reach the power of the universe, even the power of God coming up if you go deep enough. The minister sees this as a great healing energy which can be tapped and which will respond to prayers for healing, but he's frank to admit he doesn't understand it.

I myself feel that the love-energy of the universe is there for us to tap and whether we do it by biofeedback or autogenics, by prayer or healing movements, we're actually only balancing the autonomic nervous system and this balance is what ultimately must do the healing by the vast changes it produces in our system. Just a little shift and we can shift the body back from sickness to health.

Arthur Freese on the other hand looks at it somewhat differently. He sees the healing as coming about as the result of psychic mechanisms—the love and warmth and deep sincerity of the healer's personality plus the ability of this healer and the situation to build up the expectation of the sufferer to a point where he actually expects a healing effect, and therefore heals himself.

I have found psychics invaluable. Their diagnoses direct me repeatedly in the handling of my patients and their problems, and I have seen their actual healings. Knowing from a psychic's insights that the source of one woman's pain was her concern over her husband's behavior, I could sit down with her and, together with our other techniques for pain relief, solve her particular problem.

With repeated instances of this sort, it's not surprising that I have Henry Rucker lecture to every group of my patients, to orient them and secure their cooperation, to move them to rethinking the cause of their pain and the problems they face personally. For chronic pain, as we shall discuss later, is usually an exaggeration of the real pain that is present—a psychological distortion of reality if you will.

In addition to this I make available to all my patients the opportunity for personal interviews and consultations with Henry Rucker. Along with other investigators in this field, I have found that the patient in pain cannot get help from the usual psychotherapy that the medical and psychological professions have to offer. But I feel that Henry with his clairvoyance can see through to the core of the problem and counsel the patients, making possible in a short time what might take years with conventional psychotherapy. I've also used different types of psychics in a variety of ways—to diagnose problems and suggest treatments, and to reveal the workings of the patients so I can zero in directly on the problem and apply the necessary medical treatments.

Of two things I am sure: that we have yet to find and prove the basis of faith healing scientifically; and that we have only one way to deal safely and successfully with this raw power: *YOU MUST UTILIZE CONVENTIONAL MEDICAL HELP— FOLLOW YOUR DOCTOR'S ADVICE AND CONTINUE HIS OR HER TREATMENTS—EVEN WHILE YOU TRY FAITH HEALING!*

I can't emphasize this point too much. Until we know all there is to know about disease of every kind and about faith healing (which times it works, when and on whom, and where and why it fails,) you *must* continue in medical care while you seek this extra dimension of healing.

Faith healing can perform miracles—it's saved lives given up for lost by conventional medicine—but when you're dealing with life itself you can't afford to take any chances. Use faith healing by all means—but use it right, as *an adjunct* to conventional medicine and *not as a substitute.*

We need a new method of medical care to protect patients while at the same time giving them and their doctors additional therapeutic tools which may be of benefit, combining both conventional medicine and the occult so that patients can gain the best of both worlds.

Let me tell you how I turned to all this—for in this story you will gain an insight into occult medicine, as well as have the opportunity to judge me, and thus judge what I have to say here and my right to speak out.

How I Came
to the Occult
in Medicine

Here is *my* story. It may seem strange to some, but there is
a rational pattern to it all, and it does move in a straight
line from the beginning to the present; from the hard
sciences such as physics to the "softer" biological and medical sciences; and finally to things of the mind, altered
states of consciousness, parapsychology, and the occult.
I've seen medically inexplicable healing produced by psychics, and scientifically unaccountable diagnoses made. I
think this all has significance and value—and promise
too—for you. And most important, I believe you have the
right to know it all.

It's not surprising that traditional medicine, with its
great age, is stiff and unyielding, no longer easily capable
of either flexibility or change. Turned conservative, this
profession of mine now condemns the radical ideas which
seem new but actually came out of the youth of the profession when emotion and love and magic were part of its

everyday practice. Those were the days when miracles were a daily commonplace, whether in a witch doctor's hut or an astrologer's attic or, later, at Lourdes. As a white-coated, scientific student and intern, I too would have sneered skeptically at these ideas. But I'm older and more experienced now—and I have actually seen medical miracles myself and I have learned of those experienced by others. I've lost my barren skepticism.

I'm certain you want to know more about *me* as well as about this healing so that you can judge for yourself.

I come of a conservative background and a most traditional scientific and medical training. For I'm descended from hard-shelled Lutherans and Baptists, spent my formative years in a small town of the Bible Belt, went to college at a neighboring Southern university and then to its medical school. I was deeply affected when I took the sacred 2,500-year-old Hippocratic oath to help and not hurt, and I've always felt my first responsibility was to heal the sick. Where this clashed with the beliefs or behavior of the traditional medical establishment, my patients' welfare came first.

So it was that after my early career of medical research and practice spent with the latest electronics and computers of our scientistic age, I found myself seeking help for my patients from ancient and mystical Chinese lore and modern psychic healers. I've seen psychics heal a large hole in the skull of a four-year-old after America's best surgery had failed repeatedly in attempts to repair it, and I've seen psychics diagnose a mysterious ailment which had baffled highly trained medical specialists. I've seen this strange kind of help heal one of my own sons and spare my wife a life-threatening medical test. Nowadays I travel a great deal, nationwide and worldwide, to lecture to physicians on varied aspects of clinical practice and occult medicine.

I was born on December 4, 1932, in Columbia, South Carolina. When I was only five my family moved the thirty miles to tiny Camden where I grew up and went to school. Camden was then a very provincial Southern town of 5,500 people (it still has only a little over 8,000) in an area where many Northerners came to enjoy the mild climate. The town itself was virtually surrounded by the huge estates of millionaires from North and South. Some of the Buckleys and one of the Woolworths had estates there and Bernard Baruch had a home there; his father had been a surgeon in what Camden still called The War Between the States.

My father was born on a farm sixty miles from Camden. He quit school in fourth grade, when his father died, and went to work as a butcher. He was a driving ambitious man from whom I think I must have gotten some of these same qualities—I hope to good purpose. He finally bought out the store where he worked, supplying it with beef from our own farm when I was eleven, and I worked in the store in the winter and on the farm in the summer.

The Camden in which I grew up was a leisurely gentle town devoted to horses and this brought in the horsey set. In April we had the Carolina Cup Steeplechase and in November the National Fox Hunt. There were also horse shows, polo, riding, and hunt meets. At sixteen I left Camden for Duke University where I attended both college and medical school. From then on, I returned to Camden only for short vacations because my summers were filled with scientific research at Duke—and once I tentatively tried Canada's McGill University for advanced biochemical research, so deep was my interest in basic science.

But it was back there, in quiet little Camden that I was first touched by the occult, a faint brush anyway—for there was more going on beneath the surface of my sleepy little town than many of its residents realized. Off in a cottage at the edge of town was a little old black woman with short gray hair and a scar shaped like a pair of hands folded in prayer on her chest. I still suspect that this scar (medically called "keloid") was produced deliberately. Beth (not her real name) was a rare clairvoyant and consulted by many people, including—it was rumored—a mayor of a neighboring town and a governor of the state. Beth was my mother's confidante and in my youth we made many trips to her. My mother must have consulted or visited Beth at least once or twice a week but to me it was all rather bizarre and I paid it virtually no serious attention.

Beth supposedly had found many lost things—and missing persons as well. Stories were told of her power (even of her solving a local crime) but most of those who visited her went there for personal advice. She was rarely without a Bible in her hands; when you asked her help she would promise to "dream on it"—and in a few days you would get her answer.

My mother had great faith in Beth, my father thought it all sheer rubbish, and I was the typical teenager with an indifferent skepticism. But just before I left for college, Beth took me down a few pegs. Responding to my mother's request for a "reading" on me, Beth said I would be "almost famous but never quite so." With this putdown I left for college where I joined the Duke Players—but Beth was right for I've never found fame—certainly not as an actor.

In the excitement of being a teenager leaving home for the first time and entering the expanding world of college, I forgot old Beth and the visits to see her. But late in my college years the Duke Players assigned me to do a radio skit (we didn't have campus TV in the early fifties) on parapsychology. For this I turned—cynically to be sure—to Duke's famous Dr. J. B. Rhine: here was truly the grand old man of the occult and of psi (a term usually preferred, to cover the whole field—parapsychology, ESP or extrasensory perception, clairvoyance, precognition, psychokinesis and the rest which I'll try to explain more fully later).

Although I came to his laboratory with a skeptical chip on my shoulder, predetermined to mock the work, Dr. Rhine's obvious sincerity and honesty along with his generous contribution of time out of an unbelievably busy schedule, began to convert me. I found myself watching his research several hours a week for months on end, and it all eroded my initial cynicism.

It had taken a quarter of a century for Dr. Rhine to develop his special deck of twenty-five cards and they are now used worldwide. This deck is unique. Each card carries a symbol: star, square, circle, cross, or three wavy lines. With this and a set of dice, Dr. Rhine struggled for half a century (the real beginnings of this work must be dated back to the 1920s) to prove scientifically that clairvoyance and mental telepathy, precognition (knowing things before they happen) and psychokinesis or PK (mind-over-matter, the mind making physical things happen) are realities; that paranormal abilities do actually exist, in some people more than others as does the ability to do mathematics or play football.

The way it all worked was most ingenious. A subject might be given a set of the cards face down and have to guess each symbol and thus go through the entire deck. Then the success rate was compared with what might have been guessed just by chance alone. Gradually, Rhine selected those people who seemed consistently to get better results than could possibly have happened by chance alone: this was clairvoyance. In telepathy, an agent or sender would concentrate on the symbol as he turned each card face up while another person (a receiver) in a distant room would try to write down the symbol. Here again the statistics seemed to indicate that some people could really do a lot better than the run-of-the-mill individual, the chance guesser.

Lastly Rhine turned to throws of the dice. Some people seemed better able than others to foretell which faces would come up most often. He had other people try to do psychokinesis—PK—to make the dice come up in certain ways by willing it with their minds.

By the time I'd completed my research for the radio skit I was sold. The figures were there; some people did actually seem to have psychic powers. I wrote that radio skit and began it with the sound of rolling dice. But I was bothered. Even though I was only eighteen, I was deeply annoyed because it seemed to me that J. B. Rhine had already proved that ESP and PK and clairvoyance and the rest were reality, that they really did happen to some people. But to continue to put all that time and money into repeating the same reading of cards and throwing of dice seemed a waste of time, utter nonsense. I just couldn't see the point of doing something with no practical application. It should be put to some use—even Beth had done that. I did not foresee the practical uses which were about to be found for it.

I told Dr. Rhine about Beth and he was interested in looking into her talents, but just about then I left for medical school. Its demands again drove all thoughts of Beth and parapsychology out of my mind. And, in fact, it wasn't until just a few years ago that the grand old man of American medicine, Dr. Paul Dudley White, threw me once more headlong into psi.

The excitement of medicine and its sciences delighted me—in fact, as early as graduation from high school I'd been attracted (almost—it occasionally seems to me now—by some mystic compelling force) to neurosurgery. I know that the strange intricate mysteries of the mind and brain have always fascinated me and medical school opened the way for me to explore the nervous system in all its complexities.

The brain is an amazing organ—almost incredible to scientists as well as laymen. It has taken some two billion years to develop this brain you use so casually and automatically every second of your life, which keeps you breathing and your heart beating, gives you sight and thought and feeling. It's jammed full of nerve cells—neurons—which are the basic building blocks of brain and mind. In your brain are approximately ten billion neurons plus another hundred billion other cells (glia cells) whose job we don't yet fully understand.

Actually your whole wonderful brain is a mere three pounds of deeply grooved and indented shiny jellylike tissue whose cells communicate through some 500 trillion cross connections (called synapses) which are not actual contacts but spaces of less than a millionth of an inch (for no nerve cell ever actually touches another in intimate embrace). These synapses act like traffic policemen to speed or slow or even halt the reports—the nerve impulses—coming from your body up through your spinal cord. Without these one-way gaps or controls, a wild flood of impulses would pour in from every whisper or sound or breath or breeze, the touch of your foot to the ground or the clothes on your body, the chair on which you sit.

Without some policing or filtering mechanism, this never-ending barrage of sensations and stimulations would likely throw you into uncontrollable epileptic seizures. But it's all handled smoothly by the thinking "you"—your gray matter, the cortex of your brain. This is a wrinkled covering of soft gray tissues a tenth of an inch or so thick and some two feet wide and three feet long. This cortex makes up roughly half the weight of your entire nervous system and a column of it the thickness of a pencil contains some 50,000 neurons while a cubic inch will hold 100 million cells.

In general your brain works through your spinal cord for—except for some nerves of the face and head which run directly into the brain—all the nerves of your body connect to the brain by way of the spinal cord. This cord is a two-way communications pathway about a foot and a half long (depending on your height). It's a soft tapering cylinder twice the thickness of a pencil. Nerve fibers run in columns here, some carrying up to the brain the story of what's happened while others bring down return messages (to make your stomach digest its food instead of tying itself in knots, for instance).

Utterly absorbed by all this, I turned to neurophysiology—how the nerve cell and the whole nervous system functions—in medical school, and my research was in this most scientific of all medical disciplines. This field is truly a technologically oriented science in which sophisticated electronics play a major role. One of its vital breakthroughs, for example, came just as I was preparing for college—the electron microscope. Here, electrons instead of light make it possible to see microscopic structures such as cells and synapses. From the original electron microscope in 1932 to its special refinement in 1945, development was as fabulous and as rapid as man's sudden conquest of space—for in little more than a decade this instrument was brought to the level of perfection it had taken 300 years for the original familiar light microscope to reach.

With these electron devices it's possible to get enlargements of a million times and more—just what you need for synapses with their millionths-of-an-inch gaps. The study of the nerves themselves calls for the most modern physics—for example, to measure the transmission of nerve impulses by checking the electrical changes that sweep along the nerve length (sometimes at speeds approaching 300 miles an hour).

In medical school I tried to learn to reach out for new ideas. I wasn't always successful, but I contributed, in my research, to the knowledge about the amygdala, a vital part of the brain concerned with emotions. Removal of the amygdala can turn even the most savage animal, such as the notorious wild rat, into a gentle placid one, or it can remove an animal's fear. But, strangely, it doesn't always work this way; sometimes it produces greater fear and more aggressiveness. We don't know why. Clearly we have only a superficial understanding of the way the brain functions and we will have to learn far more before we can safely intervene in the human brain except for such disorders as tumors or strokes or aneurysms.

However, with this new understanding of the basic role that parts of the brain such as the amygdala play, it became possible to control a human being by simply implanting electrodes in the brain and beaming electrical impulses there. Such tests are frightening, implying as they do total control over another human being's mental and emotional life. There are also the terrible dangers of psychosurgery which are only now provoking concerned reactions from the scientists and medical people who are devoted to humanity.

Dr. Jose Delgado, then of Yale University, has troubled many in the medical and scientific communities by demonstrating the ease of acquiring control over the mind. In one early experiment, for instance, Delgado descended into the bull ring carrying a red cape and armed with only a radio transmitter. When the wild bull came charging down at him, he waited until the animal was close, then pressed a button and the bull pulled up short in a cloud of dust. Electrodes had earlier been implanted in the animal's brain and these were activated by Delgado's transmitter. He also implanted electrodes in human brains to demonstrate the control that could be exerted here too. Frightening implications!

My own medical school research involved the functioning of the nervous system and led me into neurosurgery as a career. And I was thus forced to deal with that major problem—specialization—which medicine has always faced (2,500 years ago, Herodotus wrote of this same tendency among the Egyptian physicians).

One weakness of medical school training today is in the students' tendency to go directly after graduation into their future specialties without ever really learning to be good doctors. They are specialists right from the start with experience and knowledge limited to one particular field. This bothered me—and I'm glad now of my youthful caution—so I deliberately first took a general *medical* internship at Duke, where I learned about diseases and their treatment by drugs and medication, about diagnoses and the causes, where known, of the many illnesses people suffer. Then came a general surgical residency to learn *all* kinds of surgery (at St. Louis' Barnes Hospital) and only then to Massachusetts General Hospital (which gave anesthesia to the world and where the father of modern neurosurgery, Harvey Cushing, interned) for my training in neurosurgery. I still had no idea I was to turn again one day to occult and unconventional medicine.

It was actually my Duke internship which planted the seeds of doubt about conventional medicine in my mind. An internist (a specialist in general medicine) there talked to us of psychosomatic diseases (those caused primarily by emotional problems which manifest themselves in physical symptoms) such as stomach ulcers or asthma or headaches. He emphasized that 85 percent of symptoms were psychosomatic. And here—really—began my search for an alternative medicine, because if so many medical problems were emotional, why weren't we taught a way to treat emotional difficulties? It took long years to find a new way to deal with these problems—long years plus an understanding of occult alternatives.

While serving at Massachusetts General Hospital I took off

eight months to spend with Sir John Eccles in Australia. This neurophysiologist was then working on the electrical conductivity of nerves, research which in 1963 brought him a Nobel Prize. Here, too, the groundwork was laid for one of my own contributions to medicine, the electrical devices which can control pain without destructive surgery. I might have stayed on to practice in Australia, but my wife was already feeling personal stirrings of Women's Liberation and worried about the masculine-dominated society there.

At this period psychosurgery was sweeping the world. Surgeons (and even nonsurgeons) were tearing into human brains (forgetting these were living minds), cutting and burning and slashing to correct, they thought, personality and mental diseases and to wipe out pain. One early proponent was even said to be carrying out these "lobotomies" with an icepick.

Although these doctors and their radically destructive operations failed to achieve anything really worthwhile, they did succeed in turning innumerable human beings into listless and virtually human-less imitations of people. Only recently has the reaction to the terrible excesses of this surgery finally assumed powerful form. Growing numbers of physicians and allied scientists have condemned them.

I saw it all at first hand—gross, crass, irresponsible operations that could not be called medicine or surgery or research. I protested and my career was almost washed out before it had really begun. At this point I was so dismayed by psychosurgery and its ramifications that I nearly gave up neurosurgery. However, I got involved in the problems of pain and seeking new methods of controlling it without destructive cutting.

I welcomed the opportunity to join the staff of Cleveland's Case Western Reserve School of Medicine. It was here that I worked on my first venture into unconventional medicine—the electrical device to be placed on the spinal cord to short-circuit the nerve pathways and prevent pain from reaching the brain, from being "felt." My chief reacted to the unconventional in the way the medical establishment almost always does: "Ridiculous—it won't work! My God, you have some wild ideas!"

But with the confidence—or brashness—of the young, I entered the world of unconventional medicine almost on my own. A young electrical engineer and I devised and built an electrical device to outwit pain. Two years were spent on this device, with innumerable trials on experimental animals to insure first its safety and then its efficacy, to know with scientific thoroughness precisely what we could expect, and then to perfect the technique of surgical installation. Finally it was used for the first time on a human being, a man dying of cancer, and at least it gave him some peaceful moments and surcease from pain before his end. It has now been used for thousands of patients by many surgeons who participated in extensive national tests to determine the potentialities of the device. It is an alternative form of medicine, nondestructive and helpful with some patients. I'll say more of this later.

As a result of this work, I stumbled on something similar that has proven to be a highly effective bit of occult medicine (actually long known but discarded and almost abandoned). I discovered a simple electrical device which sends an electrical current through the skin to control acute temporary pain—a sprain or broken bone, a severe bruise and the like—about 80 percent of the time. And in chronic pain it can give amazing relief, even eliminating the need for the overwhelming doses of narcotics so commonly used. Converted to modern electronics, it has performed wonders and may well end up as a medicine chest item, for it is safe and harmless but very effective—a sort of electrical aspirin, maybe!

Seeking more intellectual freedom, I moved on to private neurosurgical practice in La Crosse. I maintained my academic contacts by devoting some of my time to teaching professorships at the Universities of Wisconsin and Minnesota. But surgery was beginning to interest me less and less—I really wanted to heal without cutting, if I could.

The neurosurgeon often considers himself the dumping

ground for pain problems when the regular physician can no longer deal with a troubled, distraught sufferer. Moreover, the pain-relieving devices I'd developed were bringing me many referrals. But now I was looking for a way to circumvent even this form of surgery as well.

I discovered that in Seattle a new and unconventional approach to pain was being tried, with methods almost purely psychological—operant conditioning. Dr. Wilbert E. Fordyce, a clinical psychologist, breaks the pain habit by paying warm attention to increased activity and decreased pain complaints. Complaints of pain and failure to carry out planned activities are met with noncommunication—the staff pays no attention to this patient. (I'll explore this, too, in detail later.)

I adopted this approach, as well as physical aids (such as electrical skin devices, cold, massages, etc.) and so my original Pain Clinic was founded. Here people came who were so disabled by their pain that they sometimes spent twenty-three hours of the day in bed. Typically, these were people who had been turned into addicts by the drugs given too freely by doctors who were trying mistakenly—and unsuccessfully—to relieve chronic pain. The results have been dramatic. People have been restored to normal lives in which they are once more of value to themselves, their families, and their communities. They are no longer dependent on drugs.

Then came the breakthrough into the world of the occult. I actually owe it to one of the classic and most admired and beloved figures in the medicine of this century, that magnificent old man of medicine, that proper Bostonian (by birth, training, and career), Dr. Paul Dudley White. When I was testing out needle electrodes for the control of pain in local nerves, it was suggested this was the Western equivalent of acupuncture—and Dr. White, who never missed anything in his beloved profession, asked me to meet him. He wanted to discuss my work and how it related to the acupuncture which he'd seen when he was one of the first American physicians to visit Red China.

I flew to Boston in 1972 and we had a private meeting. He

was eighty-six then, and only a year away from his death. He was a true doctor, who treated his humblest patient no differently from Pablo Casals or President Eisenhower. The day he saw me he flew in from a two- or three-week trip to Europe, saw a patient immediately on his return from the airport, and then spent several hours with me. We discussed his Chinese experiences and what he knew of acupuncture, and talked about my electrical stimulation work that had—literally!—sparked our meeting. We didn't finish until about seven o'clock. I would have been absolutely bushed after such a day, but Dr. White was still bubbling with energy as I left him.

It was this visit with Dr. White that threw me into parapsychology for the first time since Dr. Rhine and Duke University. Three weeks after our meeting, I got a call from the Academy of Parapsychology and Medicine: Dr. White, who had been supposed to speak on acupuncture at their meeting, had suggested that I could do it better. He joined the panel discussion after my presentation but refused to give a formal paper because he felt that I was better informed. This was typical of his complete lack of conceit.

At this time I knew virtually nothing about psi. Suddenly there was a new world of unconventional and occult medicine opening before me and all I wanted to do was to explore it, to probe its hopes and limits.

It was very strange at first and I admit that I found some difficulty in freeing myself from my conventional medical thinking. But as the scientist I hoped I was, I felt I had no choice: if there was a possibility that I might find something of benefit, I had to do it.

There were facts that I hesitated to believe or accept simply because I'd laughed at them most of my life—such as psychic healing and psychic diagnosis. For example, a patient of mine, while sitting in my reception room, "had a feeling" that her father—a healthy man in his fifties—was "in trouble." She couldn't be more specific, but because she was so upset I saw her ahead of her turn so she could get home sooner. An hour or so later she called me. She'd had a phone call that her father had had a serious heart attack. (Almost all of us have had similar psychic insights.) Then there was the patient—a man of nearly sixty—who told me that a laying-on-of-hands by one of our well-known psychic healers had relieved the pain of a slipped disc and freed him to lead a normal life.

It was instances like these that made things both different and difficult for me. To be faithful to medicine and to my belief that it was my responsibility to help and heal but not hurt my patients, I felt I had to explore the occult.

There was evidence that faith healing did work, at least some of the time. And so it was that the occult lured me on.

There was evidence of psychic powers not explainable by any of the sciences I knew. But we also can't explain how anesthetics work, and yet I wouldn't do surgery without them. And we can't explain why sugar pills have always worked. I felt I had to learn more.

As a start, I located a clairvoyant psychic, Henry Rucker of Chicago. He told me things about myself I don't think anyone had ever known before. I virtually dared him to participate in a test at my hospital in La Crosse. He would bring a team of some half-dozen psychics from his Psychic Research Foundation to see what they could tell by merely observing certain patients over a weekend in January 1973. They could have the patients' birth dates, palm prints, and samples of handwriting. They could see either the patients or their photos. But they could not have access to any medical data, or speak with either patients or hospital personnel. They accepted—and the results of that weekend shook me out of my remaining complacency.

Henry Rucker and his fellow psychics agreed that one man had a degenerative disease of the lymph system, and would have a crisis late in the year. Not until this patient died in October was it possible for the medical specialists to diagnose the problem as cancer of the lymph system.

The psychics stated that one patient had a nonmalignant liver problem, and predicted that he would be home within ten days. I was certain that they were wrong. We thought he had cancer. Clearly he was moribund—you had only to look at him to see it. But we found that he did have liver failure and not cancer. Only three days later he felt so well that he asked when he could go home. We sent him home within a week.

One teenager, whose terrific headaches we had failed to explain, was seen by the psychics who detected that the underlying problem was a sexual difficulty. With this information we were able to reach him through psychological means and the headaches cleared up.

My own son Brock had three large warts on his hand for six years despite care by an excellent dermatologist. Henry Rucker just sort of waved at them and said they would be gone in three weeks—and they were.

At this time a distraught couple brought their four-year-old child to me: she had fallen and fractured her skull three years before. In 99 percent of such cases, the fracture simply closes up and heals. Here the hole had grown and three operations had failed to close it. Now an inch wide by three or four inches long, the hole was expanding as the brain pushed through it. An excellent neurosurgeon had advised a fourth operation since after such a lapse of time it would be virtually impossible for the hole to be closed in any other way. I suggested we try Henry Rucker since we had nothing to lose. Henry simply took a *photo* of the child I brought him, waved his hands around it and mumbled some words I couldn't understand. Within three weeks I could feel some bone growing in around the edges of the defect. Henry saw the child just once then and did what he had with the photo originally, asserting that the child would be all right in six months. Six months later, new bone had covered the entire defect, although it was still a thin layer. It seemed almost impossible that this could have happened spontaneously. I could only think—and wonder.

My own wife was spared a dangerous brain X-ray which was recommended by every neurosurgeon we consulted. Henry said the condition would clear up and the test was unnecessary. We did nothing and the condition did clear up. True, about 20 percent of the time this condition does clear up spontaneously. Was she just one of the lucky ones? I don't know, frankly.

There is much more, as you will see. These psychics were 98 percent accurate in pinpointing the emotional makeup of patients, 80 percent accurate in diagnosing physical conditions, just on that single weekend. Impressed, I decided to try to prove it all. I prepared a questionnaire for the psychics to fill out on selected patients, so that we could computerize their responses and check their diagnoses against what we already knew from medical and laboratory tests. We were thus able to scientifically determine the accuracy of these psychics in medical diagnoses and in describing the emotional and psychological makeup of our patients. I was particularly interested in the physical diagnoses since their accuracy is easier to check than emotional ones.

The objective scientific proof of the value of psychics in diagnosis—the most basic problem of medical practice—is here and you'll find a detailed account in my last chapter. The psychics' records have proven virtually equal to those of highly trained physicians with all their laboratory backup. But think how valuable it would be for doctors to have the occult to support them in their decisions in the many uncertain areas of medical care—as in cases like my wife's, where dangerous tests were being considered (and certain of the tests done on the heart or brain, or those procedures needed to permit special types of X-rays to be taken, are dangerous or even life-threatening).

As to psychic or faith healing, psychiatrists are now beginning to discern, however dimly, the scientific reasons why it happens. For the first time there is the glimmering of a truly objective in-depth understanding of something which has been going on for perhaps three million years.

Certainly there have always been miracles in medicine and at least part of the miracle, I continue to be convinced, is love. In fact, I'm quite certain that what made the old-fashioned family doctor—the general practitioner of the pre-World War II generations—such a beloved and hallowed figure was simply the love he gave so freely. And love, transmitted in the laying-on-of-hands, was most of what the old G.P. could bring to the battle against disease for there were few effective drugs, medications, or technology at the time. But the patient brought something too—faith in the doctor. In the occult world there is much talk of the energy that the psychics concentrate with their hands—and perhaps this energy too is only love, drawn from the faith on both sides.

I've lectured to physicians around the world and been an invited lecturer or visiting professor at some eighteen medical schools here and abroad during the last three years—and I've consistently found a strange fear, almost a phobia, in my profession: doctors are terrified by the word "occult." Many doctors carry out all the practices of occult medicine and will readily attest to the fact that love or faith or some religious or other-worldly power makes the difference between life and death repeatedly in their practices. Yet they shrink before the word "occult" which somehow frightens them. Perhaps they fear the possibility of ridicule by their colleagues. But I am pleased to see that this fear is beginning to disappear. Growing numbers of my professional colleagues are finally recognizing the facts we explore in this book. They are becoming intellectually honest with themselves and beginning to use accurate terms—even if the term is "occult medicine."

4

Occult Medicine: History and Development

Actually, the occult is very new—and very old. It's as new as this morning's newspapers or university courses in witchcraft or the Ph.D. nurse who has just proved that the laying-on-of-hands can raise a person's hemoglobin level for six months or more. But it's also as old as the first people who scrambled around on two legs when the world was young, or the witch doctor whose painting (apparently humanity's oldest surviving one) has been buried deep on the walls of a cave in Southern France for more than 20,000 years.

To understand, we have to go far back into the mists of time that surround, obscure, and confuse what went on when people first began living in groups and communicating with each other. *Homo Erectus,* nearly a million years ago, had a brain virtually the size of ours along with other modern characteristics: upright stature and thigh bones constructed like ours. They used stone tools, with which they cut and chopped. Many believe they could kindle fire. They may even have joined together to hunt. A recent report of another anthropological find by one of the famed Leakey family would seem to indicate that humanity may go back three million years to an ancestor of old *Homo Erectus* with a brain as large— and humanity will probably soon be declared even older.

But humanity has always suffered disease and discomfort. Almost a million years ago, a so-called "Java man" had a bony tumor of the thigh, and there is abundant evidence of other diseases in the earliest of people. At about this time or shortly thereafter, ancient people—witch doctors, medicine men, and shamans—began trephining skulls and amputating fingers.

The early trephining was really wild surgery. We have one ancient skull in which a quarter of the entire top of the head has been drilled away, and another with five holes efficiently drilled into it. Trephining could have been done for a variety of reasons: to relieve the pressure of a fractured skull (and there must have been many in those savage days); to allow the escape of the entrapped demons which were supposedly causing convulsions or epilepsy or headaches or depression; or perhaps simply to serve some religious or ceremonial purpose with which we're still unfamiliar.

What has always astonished me about this surgery is that these early occult (for religion is part of the occult, as we shall see) neurosurgeons were actually able to succeed. Even today with all our highly evolved sterile surgical techniques, anesthetics, blood transfusions, and powerful antibiotics, we still lose a relatively high percentage of patients when we have to open the skull. But those ancient surgeons—who hacked and sawed with crude stone tools, without sterilization or anesthetics—somehow managed to bring patients through alive. These old skulls show that actual healing of the bony edges took place. But those early surgeons were special, and to begin to understand them we must know something about the role of the occult in medicine.

Everybody today, it seems, is into the occult: borrowers keep the library shelves stripped bare of books on it; increasing numbers of bookstores exclusively devoted to such books open and flourish; colleges offer courses on numerology, astrology, and witchcraft— and students regularly fill them. Oakland University gave extra course credits to students spending a month in Guyana to observe a native healer, and guest lecturers included this healer and the head of the Nigerian witch doctors' association. In New York City adult education courses in witchcraft and the occult sciences are offered and there are similar courses all across the country. Sometimes these are serious; sometimes they are just plain gimmickry to exploit the students' often blind attraction to the word occult.

But despite all this exploding interest, I often wonder how many actually know what the occult is. The word comes from the Latin meaning "to conceal": the occult is hidden or arcane knowledge; things mysterious and inscrutable; information limited to the very special or informed few, the initiate. It usually implies the supernatural as well. To some, the occult is not only hidden but also rejected knowledge: information that has been discarded or refused or disbelieved. Initiates feel that the occult is rejected either because it represents a threat to the establishment and to society and its lifestyle, or because society is too blinded by its own prejudices and ignorance to see the truth. But the establishment itself feels that it rejects the occult only because it was long ago disproved. We can't settle the dispute here. Our present concern is with the role of the occult in its broadest sense—and in medical and health care.

The occult (the "occult sciences" as some put it) covers a whole range of studies. Virtually all the psi phenomena, acupuncture, astrology, alchemy, herbology, the Cabala, ritual magic and witchcraft, palmistry, clairvoyance and ESP, and faith healing are occult. Today even religion is taking a sharp turn toward the miraculous and the magical, the supernatural and the mysterious, and away from the rational and intellectual.

One can be drawn to some aspects of the occult and not to others. The occult is a mighty mixed grab bag from which you can take almost anything that attracts you. Our interest is in one spe-

cific aspect of this once hidden but now visible and vocal movement—occult *medicine*.

The Book of Genesis provides one of the first written examples of occult medicine, the formation of Eve, when God put
Adam into a deep sleep (the first anesthetic) to do a quick rib removal and then turned that bone and cartilage into Eve.

Actually, though, medicine has been occult since its very
beginning—and the occult has essentially *been* medicine. There
has been a relatively short lapse during which Western science
controlled medicine and healing, twin arts which are once more
returning to the methods of those who founded them.

The Great Mother is believed by many anthropologists to
have been the head of the primeval family. She was priest and sor-
cerer and witch doctor. To her were brought the sick and the
ailing and she performed her healing rituals, her magic. In time
she was replaced by the medicine man, the shaman, who took
over and used incantations and magic spells to drive out the
demons which brought disease and suffering, and who was perhaps
the predecessor of the priest more than of the physician. But even
with this change, the woman remained the lay healer (and many
faith healers today are women). In short, she was the ancestor of
the physician. When King Arthur of English legend was mortally
wounded it was his sister Queen Morgan le Fay who came to take
him to Avalon where she would heal him. Right from the beginning, part of the whole healing art was the use of amulets and
sacred charms, tattoos and talismans (special things worn or kept
in the dwelling-place such as rings, goodluck pieces, religious
relics, or parts of animals, like our old friend the rabbit's foot).

So right from the start, medicine was known to only a very
few initiates. Witch doctors and shamans often passed their knowledge and secrets down in families just as there are families now in
which generation after generation become physicians. Deeply
over- and under-laid with the supernatural, medicine has most
often depended on magical and mysterious rituals and we still
speak of particularly potent and effective medication (the antibi-

otics for example) as "miracle drugs" and the successful physician or healer as a "miracle-worker." To most laymen, all medicine and surgery are still miraculous. And, indeed, all medicine is faith healing, I believe.

The primeval shaman or medicine man or witch doctor still carries out his tasks today with very little change in many primitive tribes. Here we can see how he uses the occult, sometimes working with magic and sorcery and herbs to drive the demons out of his patients' bodies, sometimes falling back on such devices as shooting tiny arrows into the victim and sucking out the evil. But often, too, there is a talking-out of problems in a primitive sort of psychotherapy (or maybe we should say psychotherapy is only a modern form of witchcraft).

When the Code of Hammurabi was set down around 4,000 years ago, its material was already old and perhaps even ancient. In the Code, the word for physician means "healer." Surgeons and physicians were differentiated, with the surgeon carefully regulated while the priest-physicians were left to practice freely. Demons were still regarded as the source of disease and incantations were the standby for the priest-physicians.

The ancient Egyptians were praised by Homer himself more than 3,000 years ago for their advanced medicine. They too began with priests. In fact, the Egyptians' knowledge of anatomy was gained by the priest-physicians who prepared bodies for embalming. Imhotep, the first physician we can see clearly through the confusing lack of historical records, was an Egyptian of some 5,000 years ago. He became the Egyptian god of medicine, but during his lifetime he was priest, physician, astronomer, and magician (an ideal combination for occult medicine!).

The two oldest medical papyri—the Edwin Smith and the Ebers (named for the scholars who purchased them in Egypt in 1862 and 1873)—date back some 5,000 years and tell of medical practices and concepts that were ancient even then.

The Edwin Smith Papyrus is the oldest scientific surgical treatise we have. The word "brain" is written for the first time (along with information on the paralyses that result from damage to various parts of the brain). Here too is the first recorded recognition of the pulse and the role the heart plays in blood circulation—amazingly close to the principles of the circulation of the blood which were described by William Harvey in 1628.

The papyrus of Ebers tells of the three types of ancient Egyptian healers: the physicians who used remedies or medication; the surgeons who operated on wounds, fractures, dislocations, and the like; and, finally, the sorcerers who utilized exorcisms, amulets, spells, and the magic arts.

The Aztecs of this continent developed a degree of specialization equal to that of the Egyptians. Both the Egyptians and the Aztecs relied heavily on the supernatural and the use of prayers along with a collection of varied materials or objects having magical healing powers.

Ancient Greeks and Romans also sought medical help from priests, who put sufferers to sleep in a temple, to heal and restore them.

One of our most recent medical tools is the use of electricity in the control of pain. When I first developed my electrical device to short-circuit pain in the spinal column, and the simpler device to apply to the skin, I thought they were original. But when I looked into occult history, I was stunned to find that these most modern devices with their transistorized electronics and latest technology were actually known and used some 5,000 years ago! For the Egyptians have pictures of an electric fish—a living electric battery—on the walls of one of their ancient tombs. The numbing powers of this electricity (some of these fish put out enough to knock a horse down) were known to the earliest writers and the ancient name of the fish showed this knowledge. Plato and Aristotle wrote about this fish's ability to numb with its electric shock some 2,500 years ago. The ancients used nature's own biological electricity for headaches, gout, epilepsy, and childbirth. It was all unconventional medicine, then as now.

The Hebrews of the Old Testament, some 3,000 years ago set up excellent public health and sanitation laws and mixed these with the occult—a blend of religion, medicine, and mysticism.

The Prophet Elijah was brought a boy who had just died. The prophet—as you can read in the Bible—threw himself on the lad and breathed the breath of life back into him. It all sounds amazingly like our recently discovered technique of CPR (cardiopulmonary resuscitation, mouth-to-mouth breathing) which has saved people who were clinically dead.

It was in this period that scientific medicine first appeared with the teachings of Hippocrates, the father of Greek medicine, who lived some 2,500 years ago. Yet even Hippocrates is thought by some to have used astrology in his practice. His interest in "critical days" may have had a basis in numerology and—I like to think—in biorhythm. Hippocrates often refers to the constellations of the stars in his writing—and to the critical days when a crisis would occur in acute illnesses.

Jesus, of course, made healing an important part of his ministry and part, too, of his charge to his disciples. The Acts of the Apostles records that Peter and John cured a lame man in the Temple, who then arose and gave thanks to God for his healing. Healing has always been part of Christianity, although it fell into disuse. However, in the past fifteen years or so it's been restored to its ancient place of honor, particularly in the Episcopal Church where the laying-on-of-hands is now an important part of the ministry.

This revival of interest started in England with Anglican ministers, and now you can attend healing services in many Episcopal Churches throughout this country. One in New York City up on Park Avenue is St. Bartholomew's Church and down on Wall Street famous old Trinity Church is another; there are leaders of this new ministry at St. Stephen's Episcopal Church in Philadelphia, and America's greatest faith healer, Mrs. Olga Worrall, conducts faith-healing services at a Methodist Church in Baltimore. Every day sees an increase in the churches involved in this basic Christian ministry, in virtually every community of any size in the United States today.

Early India, too, had its admixture of the occult and medicine. Demons and magic and the gods were all brought into play as part of the medical therapies. But they also had a surgery definitely ahead of any other of its day. For instance, they performed amazing plastic surgery, rebuilding noses, which had been cut off as punishment for adultery, and repairing ears and lips.

The ancient Chinese healing methods are much more familiar to Americans today with our increased interest in acupuncture (based on the mystic theories of *Yin* and *Yang*) in herbology, and in other aspects of the varied occult practices that form the traditional Chinese medicine which has now been wedded to their Westernstyle scientific medicine.

In Europe at this time, Rome was at its height and Galen was the great Roman physician of the second century after Christ. His work influenced the practice of medicine more than that of any other physician in all history. For some 1,500 years his words were seen as inviolable, even infallible. But Galen too used the occult in his choice of drugs, and he turned to his own dreams to know the future course of a disease and how to treat it. In fact, Galen originally studied medicine because of a dream about his father. He even recognized psychosomatic medicine, for he tells of the depressed woman whose pulse suddenly beat fast at the mention of a theatrical idol of the day, a handsome male dancer.

By 500 A.D., Europe had already entered the Middle Ages, what the scientist and the physician sometimes call the Dark Ages—for while much intellectual and cultural activity was then going on, medicine and science either slipped backward or simply relied on quoting the great figures of the past to dismiss any new concepts. The greatest medical figure in this period was across the Mediterranean, the Arabian Rhazes, and he too was deep into occult theories involving alchemy, theology, and philosophy.

The Middle Ages brought with them to Europe a series of wars, the Crusades, supported by the Papacy and aimed at those it regarded as enemies of Christ. When the first Crusaders captured Jerusalem in 1099 they found a Christian hospital waiting there for them. It had been established by monks who formed the Knights of St. John or the Hospitallers. Their black habit with its eightpointed cross identified the first nursing order—one which lasted for nearly a thousand years. Once more the occult (in the broader sense in which I use this term) and religion had made their mark on medicine. The Crusades had their share of miracle cures, too.

The Benedictine Monastery at Monte Cassino in Salerno, Italy, became the center for miraculous cures. The most famous was that of the Emperor Henry II who, supposedly in agonizing pain from a kidney stone, fell asleep at Monte Cassino. St. Benedict appeared to the king in his dream, removed the stone surgically and healed the wound completely so that when the monarch woke he was well. In short, an early bit of psychic surgery.

During the Middle Ages, the physician followed astrology as unquestioningly as the priest followed the Gospel itself. Alchemy, too, flourished and the supernatural always seemed close at hand to help the struggling tormented masses and their frightened uncertain overlords. After the Black Death had swept all through Europe, the Dancing Mania struck. Probably a form of mass hysteria, this mania affected large crowds of men and women who would suddenly start to dance deliriously in the streets for hours on end, hand in hand. Starting in Aachen, it spread to Liège, to Utrecht and Cologne and Metz, then moved southward to Strasbourg and finally down into Italy. It took the occult to break the back of this mania, with exorcism, masses, and other religious measures taken by the clergy.

Then one of the great classic patterns of faith healing took shape. In 496 A.D., King Clovis of France was unhappy at the illness of a favorite page. He dreamed that an angel told him to put his hands on the page's neck, saying, "I touch thee and God heals thee!" Clovis obeyed and, according to Thomas Aquinas, the page was healed. Thus the Royal Touch became an accepted tool of healing for some ten centuries in England and France, and the physician to France's King Henry IV reported that the king had healed as many as 1,500 subjects at a single touching session. Today this laying-on-of-hands is again being pursued with great seriousness.

The Renaissance brought with it a change in medicine and a greater interest in what we know as scientific methods, particularly in anatomy and actual dissections. The Age of Reason was approaching and with it came a gradual reduction in the role of the occult in medicine.

However, some of the occult medicine of antiquity still survives in our own conventional medicine. The ancient Babylonians, 4,000 years ago, worshipped Marduk, god of their nation, chief god of the city of Babylon, and often invoked in incantations and exorcisms as the god of medicine. Sufferers thanked him in a poem for his help. And you too know Marduk well because every time your doctor gives you a prescription he or she too is invoking that ancient god—for the ℞ emblem on your doctor's prescription blanks is actually Marduk's symbol and was used as an invocation on the prescriptions of the physicians of Babylon many thousands of years ago.

But what of our own hemisphere, the early Americans and their medicine? The most highly developed civilizations in the Americas at the time of the early Christian era were in Central and South America—the Aztecs, Incas, and Mayas. The supernatural played a major role in their medicine and their physicians utilized incantations and magical charms or dances as did so many other peoples. The Spanish invaders who conquered the Aztecs found two classes of doctors—physicians and sorcerers—plus a whole array of specialists. There were sorcerers, for example, who were a mixed conglomeration of practitioners (in our own terms, these were psychics whose chief interest was precognition and who could foretell the future, including the diseases to come and how they would terminate); astrologers; and a group who threw corn kernels into water or onto the ground like dice, basing their medical predictions on the way the grains acted. In short, the Aztec religion was truly occult practice with mysticism its outstanding feature.

In North America, the Indians turned to their medicine men or shamans for help with their ailments. And what they were offered was typical occult medicine. In many cases the medical practitioners were actually specialized. Some acted as priests while others were herbalists or truly "medicine" men. Those with precognitive or clairvoyant gifts predicted the future or showed hidden truths. Some dispensed magic potions to make the taker powerful in hunting or wisdom or love.

North American Indians and Europeans meant different things by "medicine." Europeans meant a medication or drug; Indians meant anything (herb or object or animal, for example) which might have a therapeutic or occult significance. So the Indians fasted, prayed, and in general entered what we would now call an altered state of consciousness, and called that "making medicine." A boy preparing to enter manhood made medicine. And many of the medicine men were not only priests but chiefs as well—like Sitting Bull, Cochise, and Geronimo.

Although Indian "medicine" left its mark on our medical quackery, many Indian herbs or potions had real therapeutic value. Those taken from the willow tree are still used as aspirin.

In the nineteenth century, Americans were virtually addicted to patent medicine and were more likely to turn to this than to the local doctor, who probably had, at best, a mail-order degree, for academically trained physicians were only to be found in the large cosmopolitan cities. "Indian" doctors, self-styled "professors" and "herb doctors" traveled about the country peddling themselves or their wares from the backs of every imaginable vehicle. They sold Kickapoo Oil and Seminole Medicine, Pocahontas or Creek or Hiawatha Remedies. Innumerable so-called Indian Medicine Shows toured the country continuously.

But this was in the nineteenth century. The eighteenth century had been a period during which the growing understanding of the physical sciences and the first hints of the biological ones made mankind drunk with the heady possibilities that appeared to have opened. It seemed that soon humanity would understand everything, itself included, and that this would be done in the best of all possible worlds—one where logic and science would determine humanity's way. The future looked clear and rational. This was the new intellectual era which produced such leaders of the American Revolution as Benjamin Franklin and Thomas Jefferson.

It also produced, across the seas in Austria, Franz Anton Mesmer, a mystic and a physician who believed in astrology. He went on to convince himself that his own hands held a healing magnetic power which in 1775 he named "animal magnetism." The conventional medical profession drove him out of his homeland and he settled in Paris where he became fabulously successful. Marie Antoinette even offered him a large lifelong pension and a house, but Mesmer rejected the offer.

Mesmer's patients would sit in a circle holding hands and grasping an iron rod connected to a tub in the center of the group. Mesmer would then enter, clothed in a magnificent lilac silk robe. With a rod he was carrying would touch a person, who would promptly begin to twitch while the others too would usually become restless and disturbed. This strange "crisis" would then permit Mesmer to turn on his "animal magnetism" and "cure" the sufferers. The process became known as "mesmerism" and the French king ordered an investigation by a commission which included Benjamin Franklin. This group could find no proof of any magnetism and concluded it was all a result of imagination.

Lafayette, however, was enthusiastic about mesmerism and brought it to America with him. The French Revolution drove Mesmer out of both practice and Paris. The movement spilled over into England where a leading London physician and teacher took up mesmerism only to be driven from his professorship at the London University College Hospital in 1840 because he wouldn't give it up.

With all this fervor, it wasn't surprising that mesmerism found a welcome in the wide-open American society where Indian herb doctors or phony professors or other questionable characters had no difficulty in hawking their wares. Mesmer was accused of engaging in magic (by the Austrian medical establishment) and of being a charlatan and imposter (by the French) but mesmerism was to lead, by many devious—even questionable—paths to Christian Science and to modern hypnotism, a respectable tool of psychiatry. Despite Mesmer's total lack of understanding of his own discovery, most authorities today feel he was at least sincere in his belief in his tool—and in the right hands it did work.

Mesmerism lent itself readily to the overly free and charlatan-filled early nineteenth-century medicine of America, where stage performers used ether and nitrous oxide (the "laughing gas" dentists still use) as the psychedelic drugs of their day. "Professors" and "doctors" went about demonstrating mesmerism to the public purely as show-biz. And these stage demonstrations were everywhere.

In the mid-nineteenth century, Andrew Jackson Davis attended a demonstration of mesmerism in Poughkeepsie, New York. He began to practice medicine—for it could be done just that lightly in those days. Davis claimed that in the trance state he could diagnose illnesses (bodies were supposedly transparent to him in this state). He got involved in virtually the entire occult of his time, including naturopathy, spiritualism, clairvoyance, seances, and the rest. He also managed to write a flock of books and came to be known as the "Seer of Poughkeepsie." But his prescriptions sound like something from the Witches in *Macbeth*: frog's skin, camomile flowers, oil from the bodies of certain animals.

Rather similar in many ways is the story of Phineas Parkhurst Quimby, the son of a blacksmith, who had virtually no schooling—but did attend a lecture on mesmerism in Maine. After some playing with mesmeric medicine, he decided he could cure people better by talking with them and was soon practicing faith healing with a good bit of the occult thrown in. He even talked of what sounds remarkably like the "aura" today's psychics speak of. Believing—or at least claiming—that he had discovered Christ's own secret of healing, Quimby developed a sizeable reputation. Patients came from all over the country. One was a woman who suffered constant back pain of many years' standing. This woman was Mary Baker Eddy and she was deeply impressed with Quimby. With him, she got relief from her pain and was converted to his belief that his was Christ's secret of healing.

While Christian Science may seem a long way from Mesmer and animal magnetism, many believe that the religion came into being through this disciple of mesmerism, Quimby. When Quimby died, Mary Baker Eddy's back trouble recurred—but now she had Quimby's concepts to use as she wished. With these and the study of the New Testament, she found relief once more from her backache—and founded her Christian Science Church. Perhaps more than any other religion, Christian Science employs faith or spiritual healing and is truly occult. It has grown because of its healing powers, which have been both lauded and condemned—as has all other faith healing.

What is perhaps the oldest, greatest, and best-known center of cures is to be found in Southern France. Here is the small but world-renowned city of Lourdes, with a population in 1962 of less than 16,000. Here, between February 11 and July 16, 1858, Bernadette Soubirous supposedly saw the Virgin Mary eighteen times. Things have changed recently there; in 1958 the underground basilica of Pope St. Pius X, large enough to hold 20,000 people, was completed. Huge as it is, the basilica is really needed, for more than 2,000,000 pilgrims a year travel to this shrine in hopes of a miraculous healing either for themselves or for someone else on whose behalf they have come.

The cures at Lourdes are probably the most fully documented and thoroughly scrutinized of all faith healings in humanity's long history of the wonders of the natural and the supernatural. So intense is the Church's investigation that Lourdes probably produces far more cures than are actually accepted, simply because of the almost unbelievably rigid requirements to be fulfilled before the Church calls one a miracle. John Camp in his recent book, *Magic, Myth and Medicine*, lists the criteria: the disease must have been very serious and difficult to cure; there must have been no chance of spontaneous remission; medical treatment must have failed; cure must be prompt or sudden and complete but not natural; and there must be no relapse. While he reports that fewer than sixty cures have been recognized by the Catholic Church as miraculous, the no-relapse rule alone would seem to require that the person be dead before the healing could be recognized.

For example, Camp tells of a World War I soldier with cut nerves and total paralysis in his right arm, a brain wound which left him an epileptic, no feeling in either leg, no physical control of bodily functions, and a hole in his skull from brain surgery.

Doctors felt he couldn't survive the trip to Lourdes but he finally got permission under careful medical supervision. At Lourdes, the epilepsy disappeared, he got back the use of his legs and his bodily functions—and the hole in his head disappeared! There was no medical explanation and three years later he was still healthy and looking toward work as a coalman. Despite this clear proof, the Catholic Church still refuses to accept it as a miraculous healing.

But in any case, a widely quoted saying is unquestionably true. Regardless of what happens, whether there is a cure or not, "the trip to Lourdes is never made in vain." To understand this, to appreciate the miracles of Lourdes one must, I believe, accept the possibilities of faith healing, accept the fact that we do not yet know how mind affects body—but that we know it does—for better and worse. If we accept that mind can produce illness (psychosomatics), I think we must accept that mind can produce health—and healing. It makes sense to me.

Today's world is filled with faith healers. Some are charlatans, some merely try tentatively, others give serious effort and still fail. But there are also many—Mrs. Olga Worrall, Henry Rucker, Dr. Lawrence LeShan, Kathryn Kuhlman, and many others—whose successes cannot be ignored, and who are recognized by some distinguished members of the medical community itself.

Whether you want to regard it as magic or miracle or witchcraft or psi phenomenon or suggestion, faith healing does work for some and has helped in a broad range of serious disorders. This is where the most exciting aspects of the occult arise. For what could be more wonderful than healing a human being? And the ability to diagnose a person's ailments accurately is an essential part of healing. And perhaps it's this dream of accurate diagnosis that leads those of us who are at the fringes of the occult and unconventional medicine to press on with our work.

I feel very strongly that there is a place for the occult, for unconventional medicine, in our total scheme of medical and scientific healing—just as there is a vital place for conventional or traditional medicine. The relationship between these two forms of medicine—and their relationship to *you*—will be explored and explained in a separate chapter.

If the occult can help us avoid a dangerous test; if it can help heal the skull of a four-year-old so that further surgery can be avoided; if it can foretell the course of a disease or pinpoint its cause; if it can relieve suffering or just make the victim better able to live with a problem that can't be helped; if it can save even one single life—and especially if this occult is harmless and perfectly safe—then to my way of thinking it is justified.

Your Medical Guide to the Occult

Psychics, Extrasensory Perception, and Clairvoyance

The new interest in the occult has brought with it talk of psychometry, clairvoyance, the much-questioned psychokinesis (PK), extrasensory perception (ESP), precognition, and much else which was utterly foreign to most American ears until just a very few years ago. It still disturbs most of the medical profession to open a professional publication and find serious news items and articles and letters written by physicians on such topics as exorcism, psychic surgery, and the meditative disciplines.

In standard medical parlance, "occult" means hidden or concealed. "Occult blood," for example, is blood that has been so altered or concealed in some body products that it cannot be recognized except through chemical analysis. Today "occult" has become *the* word, but *The Oxford Universal Dictionary* of less than twenty years ago had no reference to the supernatural among its various definitions of "occult."

But in medicine today "occult" includes psi phenomena, ESP, astrology, and the like. Unconventional medicine (alternative medicine as I like to call it) utilizes these tools. For today, the occult is unconventional medicine.

But you've got to learn the language before you can enjoy visiting another country or hope to understand its people. So let's get down to a few basics about the occult—and the most essential of all are the people, the ones who bring the occult to the rest of us. These are variously called psychics, sensitives, or mediums— and there are many other terms which refer to particular talents. Thus, clairvoyants practice clairvoyance (the power to perceive things beyond the normal abilities of ordinary human senses such as touch, sight, or smell). Astrologers study the influence of the heavenly bodies. Psychics have so-called paranormal abilities— abilities beyond what we usually consider the "normal," to see, smell, hear, remember, and the like.

But definitions break down as we move into the science of parapsychology (the study of the paranormal—some say supernormal—abilities some persons possess). The terms in such a vague area of human accomplishment are often hard to define. We speak of psychic or "psi" phenomena (often simply psi) and ESP (extrasensory perception). You can probably get as many definitions and terminologies as there are people interested in this aspect of the human mind which today we still can perceive only dimly and distortedly.

Who are these psychics? What makes them psychic? Mankind has wondered ever since it first began to seek help from the people it elevated to the special status of shamans or witch doctors. And in all this time we still have formed no clear answers. There are those who think that anyone can develop his psychic powers to this level. Others feel that it's necessary to be born with a basic talent.

The stories of how it begins for these special people are diverse. Each psychic has a favorite example. One tells me of psychic gifts that began with a fractured skull or a concussion or other serious brain injury. Another tells me how a life-threatening illness or other great personal crisis led to the appearance of this strange psychic ability. But this is the hard way of doing it; many sensitives have been aware of their odd talent for as long as they can recall.

There are courses which are supposed to develop psychic powers. I know of one physician who during such training was able to pick up physical abnormalties of people he'd never met or even seen, whom he knew only by name and date of birth. He described their personal traits such as hair or scars and other physical characteristics with 75 percent accuracy. One well-known New York City experimental psychologist, Dr. Lawrence LeShan, has developed his own technique for teaching people to be healers. He's now experimenting with a short intensive course in which the prospective healers develop their abilities by the study and practice of a series of exercises over a five-day period.

In the British Isles, faith healers have their own organization, a sort of cross between a trade union and a medical association. The members can get both training and continuing education from this organization and membership in it provides a sort of legitimacy, a form of certification, which assures the public that the particular healer does have some standing in the field and is a serious practitioner of this art with certain qualifications, not simply a quack seeking to make quick money in a loosely organized and unlicensed field.

But the question remains: is psychic ability limited to the treasured genius or ability or talent of the sacred few or is it something of which many could become capable? Is this miracle, this unusual but human ability, something for the strange few, for the mediums and sensitives, or for every one of us to variable degrees (as the ability to play chess ranges from the schoolchild just learning the moves to the elderly man killing time with the game in the neighborhood park to Bobby Fischer)? Let's look at a few instances.

Take my associate in this book, Arthur S. Freese, and an experience he had some fifteen years ago: one Tuesday night, his brother had a dream of a shrouded figure which he had seen before but only at times of tragedy. Deeply disturbed, he returned home Wednesday morning to find my associate delirious from what a doctor was calling "migraine headache." The brother called another physician and early Thursday morning a large brain abscess was uncovered by surgery. Another few hours and it would surely have been fatal. And that's no rare instance, for at least half a dozen times a year some patient tells me of a similar warning of something serious happening and some close friend or relative becoming aware of something amiss. Many others experience such awarenesses but they may fail to recognize the significance of the occurrences and just pass them off with a simple mental shrug.

Have you yourself ever been in a strange new place and felt you knew it well; met a total stranger you felt you'd always known; been aware of some tragic event before it happened; guessed some outcome correctly when all the experts were wrong; known the unexpected final score of a ballgame before the game was played?

Scientifically inexplicable intuitions like these make believers of the most skeptical of us and make me feel that the "gift," while more pronounced in some, lies, perhaps dormant, in us all and is not "unnatural." Such occurrences make most people at least admit the possibility of actual help for life itself.

The medical profession today needs help most particularly in two areas, the diagnosis of diseases and the so-called "incurable" diseases. Even hardheaded medical scientists recognize that strange healings *do* occur and we still don't really know why.

But not all the world of the occult is mystical. There is now also the *science* of the occult, the organized study of the paranormal processes. Here is where the hard-nosed scientists will be found in the psychic world. Many scientists feel the data are there and are conclusive. (I happen to believe this fully myself, while my associate is more skeptical except about faith healing.) But at least as numerous as those who believe are those professional scientists who are inclined to feel that more proof is needed. The British however seem much more willing to accept these new concepts than we are.

There are many problems involved in obtaining conclusive

statistics in this elusive field. For one thing there are only about a dozen full-time parapsychologists in the world and scientific research has decreased for financial reasons at just the time that popular interest has risen.

The American Association for the Advancement of Science (AAAS), organized in 1848, is our most prestigious national scientific body. Every scientific group wants to be accepted for membership in this organization. Thanks to internationally famous anthropologist Margaret Mead's passionate support, the Parapsychological Association became a member of the AAAS in December 1969. A list of other famous scientists who believe in parapsychology would be unending. Perhaps the most celebrated is ex-astronaut Edgar D. Mitchell who attempted to set up telepathic communications from outer space during his Apollo 14 trip to the moon. He was part of the third astronaut team to walk on the moon, and walked on it for more than two hours. Dr. Elmer E. Green, world-famous scientist of the Menninger Foundation, is known for the first real breakthrough toward a simple cure for migraine headache; he used the occult technique of biofeedback for it. Writer Arthur Koestler gets wide mention for his committed interest in this world. Our own Defense Department, the National Institutes of Mental Health, and—appropriately—the National Aeronautics and Space Administration all take the occult so seriously as to be investigating or funding various programs with a view to their use in medical care or other national needs.

It was about one hundred years ago that the first research studies and university investigations of the occult led to the formation of the Society for Psychical Research in London in 1882. One of its founders was Sir Arthur Balfour (later Prime Minister) while three Nobel Prize winners were, at various times, presidents of the society. Three years after this organization started, the American Society for Psychical Research was also begun.

But the term "parapsychology" came into real use only with the scientifically oriented research that J. B. Rhine brought with him to Duke University where he founded his parapsychology laboratory and developed his Zener deck of twenty-five cards with their almost mystical symbols. This shifted the emphasis in psychical research from the study of individual occurrences to scientifically validated studies. A good deal of research is also being carried out throughout Europe. In Czechoslovakia and other of the Iron Curtain nations, investigations into birth control by astrological techniques—an ideal version of the old "rhythm method" of birth control—are being carried out. In Russia, men and women are said to be proving they can "read" with their fingertips by holding them over the printed page, and distinguish colors as well. In Leningrad there is a state-supported laboratory engaged in telepathic research. Other research is being done at the University of Utrecht in Holland and in Prague.

But the big problem in the field is the scientific question of "replication"—the ability of different experimenters to duplicate each other's findings, a type of confirmation traditionally demanded before the scientific community will accept any new finding or report as a verified fact. But some of the scientists in parapsychology, Dr. Lawrence LeShan for one, feel that lack of replication is a peculiarity of the field and not a reason for denying its validity. Dr. LeShan sees the problem as a unique one and regards the experimental proof of parapsychology as somewhat different from that required in other fields. He calls for a redefinition of "repeatable experiment" to allow it to apply to standardized procedure followed a given number of times on a particular person, under conditions most likely to produce the desired phenomena (say precognition or clairvoyance), and where the experimenter's expertise leads him to believe this could not happen by any known physical means.

Let us look at some of these psi phenomena, starting with ESP.

Extrasensory perception—ESP is the commonly used shorthand—covers (as does psi) much if not most of the entire field of parapsychology. Not uncommonly, ESP and psi and even parapsychology are used almost interchangeably, although technically and precisely ESP is only what it says—perception or awareness gained without and beyond the use of the ordinary senses—sight, touch, taste, smell, and hearing. Proof exists in the vast storehouse of simple, everyday human experiences and awarenesses that could not have come through the senses. Now the real question—long and often hotly debated—is whether infra-human animals, too, possess ESP.

For the answer, one need only look to ordinary experience. Animals—particularly dogs and cats—have managed to make their way back to their owners from incredible distances and over territory completely foreign to them. Many observers believe the explanation of this lies in psi ability, perhaps in precognitive or clairvoyant powers of animals. There is no experimental proof of psi in such homing activity—and I would suspect it will be a long time before we have any. But there *is* proof of psi ability in animals and it's now being accumulated on both sides of the Atlantic.

At Dr. J. B. Rhine's famous Parapsychology Laboratory at Duke University, some of the very first work on animal ESP was carried out in the early 1950s. Cats were sent down a passageway at the end of which were two plates of food; the experimenter tried by thought to influence the cat to choose a particular one. The results were "significant": statistics showed that the animal was actually influenced by the investigator's thoughts. It is a question, however, whether telepathy (transmission of the thought) occurred or the animal exhibited clairvoyance (sensed what was in the human mind). And in England, one investigator has reported success in influencing the movements of paramecia (microscopic one-celled animals) by psi, while two internationally known French biologists (who prefer unfortunately to remain anonymous) have reported both at scientific meetings and in J. B. Rhine's latest book, *Progress in Parapsychology*, how mice avoided electrical shocks in a manner strongly suggestive of psi ability, again either through clairvoyance or precognition.

The Russians in particular have a considerable amount of research going on in this area. The most impressive instance of telepathy in dogs I know of was one reported by Sheila Ostrander and Lynn Schroeder in their book, *Psychic Discoveries Behind the Iron Curtain*. A Russian animal trainer had a specially trained Alsatian dog called Mars who has virtually become a Soviet theatrical star. Mars can count and dance and even stand up and say "Mama." The Russian physiologist and scientist Bechterev passed a note of instructions for Mars to the trainer, who took the dog's head in his hands, gazed into his eyes, and then released him. Mars ran into an adjoining room where he'd never been before, looked on a cluttered table there, then on a second table, and finally on a third table crowded with papers and books he found a phonebook which he brought back in his teeth to his trainer—just what the scientist had instructed the trainer to have Mars do!

True, there has been no replication of these results by other investigators to prove beyond the shadow of a doubt that animals do have psi abilities—but the evidence seems pretty compelling to me. However, I guess we'll just have to await further proof before all doubt disappears. I myself have lived with animals all my life, first on my father's farm and now on my own 330-acre farm where I breed appaloosa horses and goats. I have several house dogs along with ducks and chickens. From my own experience, I'm inclined to believe there is some communication between people and animals that can only be explained in terms to psi phenomena. It's well known, for example, that animals can and do sense human fear of them. If the explanation of this is that animals smell a real odor not available to our senses, then I remind you that probably *all* psychic phenomena have a "real" basis—as yet unavailable to our rational understanding.

Clairvoyance has always been the most impressive stock-in-trade of psychics and those who claim mystic powers. The ancient witch doctors and shamans claimed ultimate knowledge of what was going on with people or weather or crops. For clairvoyance is the ability to perceive things which aren't known to others. Clairvoyance makes it possible for the psychic who meets somebody for the first time to tell that person intimate facts about his or her life or body known only to the mystified (and usually deeply impressed) subject. The clairvoyant psychic can be aware too of something taking place at a great distance—or know what is in a sealed envelope placed before him.

Clairvoyance also occurs in the form of clairsentience or clairaudience. Some sensitives tell me they see pictures as if on a TV screen. Some see an aura—a rim of color or light around a person, like an extra layer of skin or clothing, which reveals much to the psychic—when and where disease is present, whether the person is disturbed emotionally. Other psychics see these images in their own minds—either in black-and-white or in color, tiny or very large, or just magnified. Beth, from my own hometown, would dream her clairvoyant insights in Biblical imagery or would see a passage from the Bible. Others feel that they are floating above the ground while looking down on the whole scene. Some, like Beth, have their insights in symbolic forms. Some feel that words are being said or implanted inside their minds; this is clairsentience. More common are those who experience clairaudience—these sensitives actually hear voices which no one else can hear.

Clairvoyance particularly lends itself to medical practice—for clairvoyants can "see" things which sometimes the best medical tests fail to detect or pin down. Henry Rucker of Chicago diagnosed a "lymph degeneration" almost a year before all our sophisticated scientific and hospital tests and observations were able to pinpoint the problem. It was only when the patient died that we finally learned what Rucker "saw" before. When Henry saw three paralyzed patients he could accurately spell out the cause of each one's paralysis. At no time did Henry talk either to the patients or to any medical personnel (except me, and I was careful to reveal nothing), nor did he have any access to medical records.

So a very special promise of clairvoyance for medicine is in diagnosis. The exciting and vast potentialities here have so intrigued me that in the last chapter you will find a computerized and scientifically valid study I have made (so far as I know the first of its kind) comparing the accuracy of psychic diagnosis of both physical and emotional disorders to that of conventional doctors with all their technological capabilities. As you will see, skilled psychics can, on the whole, do as well as physicians. When Olga Worrall advised the physician-patient to have a special X-ray taken to confirm what she knew was wrong, she was also diagnosing.

Another closely related psi phenomenon is telepathy. A woman in an English seashore town was startled out of a deep sleep one morning by a severe blow on the mouth. Feeling her upper lip badly injured, she was surprised to find no blood, no evidence of any injury. Much later, she learned that at the same moment her husband had been hit and his upper lip injured by his boat tiller during an early morning sail. In New York recently, a patient undergoing psychoanalysis fell asleep on the couch and at that moment, miles away, his girl friend fell asleep unaccountably and irresistibly at her desk. There are many such instances seen or reported in a wide variety of circumstances and times and places. Sigmund Freud felt that if some of the material published on telepathy could be confirmed there would be no doubt of the reality of thought communication.

Freud himself told of a mother who in her psychoanalysis talked one day of a gold coin in her own childhood. When she got home, her ten-year-old son brought her a gold coin to hold for him! Since the boy too was under analysis, his analyst probed the question but could find no reason for the action. It just suddenly occurred to the boy that he ought to do this with a coin given him long before and then forgotten.

In the 1950s another famous psychologist, Dr. Carl G. Jung, told of an acquaintance then in Europe who saw the death of a friend (in America) in a dream. A telegram the next morning confirmed the death which had occurred an hour or so before the dream itself.

The well-known American psychic Susy Smith relates in her book, *Confessions of a Psychic*, that when traveling at eighty-five miles an hour on a New Mexico road she smelled burning rubber and slowed down. This saved her life for her rear tire blew out a few moments later. How could she have smelled *rear* tire fumes from which the car was racing away?

The 1966 edition of *Collier's Encyclopedia* tells of an R.A.F. lieutenant who was in his barracks at 3:30 P.M. when a fellow aviator came in—oddly wearing his naval cap while in flying clothes. After a few words the friend noisily left and another dropped in and they discussed the previous visitor. Later that afternoon they learned that the original visitor had been killed instantaneously in a flying accident at about 3:25—while wearing his naval cap.

There is just too much evidence—as far as I'm concerned—to be disregarded. I sincerely believe these things *do* happen. And hundreds, perhaps thousands, of these occurrences, many carefully documented and corroborated, have been published during the last century or so. The first large series of hundreds of these appeared in an 1886 book by Gurney, Myers, and Podmore, *Phantasms of the Living*.

Telepathy is essentially the ability either to transmit one's thoughts or to recognize what another person is thinking. It happens in reality and in everyday life. Many observers feel it's been proven experimentally by the results obtained with Zener cards when a sender concentrates on the card turned over, then transmits his thoughts to a receiver either in the same room or at a considerable distance.

Telepathy and clairvoyance introduce a peculiar problem for parapsychologists, for it's difficult if not impossible to separate out the overlapping possibilities. On the one hand, paranormal knowledge may be obtained when an individual sees an event and reports it telepathically or someone may pick up the thoughts telepathically. On the other hand, the person with a knowledge of this distant event may not be receiving the information telepathically but may be clairvoyant and sensing the event directly. The problem is such that some people like to apply a whole different term to the process—GESP or General ESP. Thus only if no one else on earth knew a fact (say that lightning had started a fire in a deserted forest) could one be sure that some particular knowledge came from clairvoyance and not telepathy.

Take this story from the Gurney, Myers, and Podmore book. In 1884 a woman was awakened by her son's voice calling for her. Two months later a letter told of her son's death on that night and that he had repeatedly called for her. But whether he was sending a telepathic plea for help or whether she was sensing the whole incident clairvoyantly, who can say? So far as I myself am concerned, I'm practical and realistic—I just see this as one more evidence of the reality of ESP!

6

Telepathy, Precognition, and Psychokinesis

Telepathy clearly can be useful in medicine. One possible use is in detecting what patients are really trying to say when they conceal, consciously or unconsciously, significant real facts about themselves (an emotional problem perhaps, drug addiction, or compulsive gambling). It could, for example, have been either telepathy or clairvoyance when Henry Rucker told distraught parents that their addict-son who had been incarcerated would be home soon. Actually the youngster (unbeknownst to all) had just run away from the institution. Just a day or two later he called his parents to ask if he could come home. Henry might have been clairvoyant ("seeing" where the youngster was) or telepathic (picking up what the youngster was thinking).

Astronaut Edgar Mitchell successfully transmitted telepathic messages (ESP cards) to earth from nearly a quarter of a million miles out while he was racing through space on the Apollo 14 moon mission.

But much more has been tried behind the Iron Curtain with Russian investigators trying telepathically to make subjects obey simple instructions ("cross your legs," etc.). Stalin is reported to have made extensive use of a Polish telepathic expert, Wolf Messing. According to Ostrander and Schroeder in their book, *Psychic Discoveries,* Messing could telepathically control people. All the guards at Stalin's villa let him pass (he was mentally telling them "I am Beria"). He appeared in front of Stalin, who had ordered this test of the psychic's powers. Another time, Messing passed three sets of guards who had been ordered to keep him in a room and even left the building without a pass!

Closely allied to telepathy is something called by the rather odd term "psychometry." Although this sounds like mental measurements (psychometrics) it's actually far from it. For psychometry is the virtually magic ability to take an object and, just from holding it, be able to tell voluminous details of its history and that of both its present and its past owners.

It is reported that some fifty years ago a psychic was given a slip of paper that had once washed up in the Azores in a bottle. It was folded and sealed repeatedly. Buried deep in the folded paper were just a few words about a ship sinking. It was signed "Ramon." Without unfolding or unsealing the paper, the psychic described the writer even to a forehead scar (later confirmed by Ramon's widow). The psychic described how the author had sealed the missile in a bottle and thrown it overboard in one last gesture. Only Ramon's widow had known the story of the note and had offered it as a test to the psychic. Ramon had gone down with the *Lusitania* but had tossed this last communication for his wife into the sea. It had finally reached her by way of the Azores.

Psychometry is often considered a form of telepathy since it can be a means for contacting persons in distant countries. I myself know a Southern-based psychic who specializes in taking a piece of paper with a dried drop of blood on it (even a hair can be used) and from it reading out the donor's blood chemistry. I sent her a drop of dried blood on a slip of paper and got back a detailed analysis of the blood chemistry: precise amounts of sodium, potassium, blood urea nitrogen, creatinine, cholesterol—a list of nearly fifty values, in fact.

Actually this woman was a clairvoyant who just drifted into this odd specialty. Many psychics do have specialties, particularly those in the field of medicine. A witch told my associate that witches who heal specialize in certain types of diseases just as physicians do, taking on the problems with which they feel most successful or competent such as those of the skin, or diabetes. One particular witch specializes in incurable diseases.

Our Southern psychic with the ability to determine blood chemistry from a drop of dried blood was originally a medical laboratory technician. She discovered that she could provide the data with her clairvoyant ability without the usual laboratory procedures—simply by holding the bit of paper with the dried blood. The most amazing thing to me was her consistent accuracy of 75 percent—for I had her findings checked by a top-notch hospital-based medical laboratory with the normal techniques. Was there any faking? Could there have been a laboratory analysis of the blood? Not that I can possibly imagine. Medically and scientifically there is no known way for any laboratory to analyze a dried drop of blood on a slip of paper days after the sample has been obtained, days during which the blood, untreated, simply lies in a package in changing temperatures as our inadequate mails slowly transport it from La Crosse to the southeastern tip of the United States.

The potential medical uses of such a sensitive are truly enough to boggle the mind (and "boggle" is the right word here, coming as it does from the Welsh word for ghost or the Cornish one for the devil!). But this experience has been only one in a series of events which finally led me to the revolution in my thinking which led to this book—and to my concept of a new type of practice which will provide the public with a hitherto undreamed-of health protection, the holistic healing center.

Very close to clairvoyance and telepathy and psychometry is another aspect of psi: precognition. This is the capacity for knowing ahead of time, for predicting or foretelling some future event such as what decision a person will make about his life or where he will move his business. In medicine it can provide information on what will develop later into a particular difficulty—a sort of diagnosis-before-the-fact, as it were. It is also valuable in planning treatment since you can anticipate the reaction as well as future developments.

Precognition in fact is the real "sixth sense" or "clinical sense" that some unusually brilliant diagnosticians have. A famous elderly American diagnostician (a household name across the land) urged surgery for one of his patients whose unbearable abdominal pain had been put down as malingering because X-rays revealed no disease. The physician insisted on being present at the surgery and when the surgeon found nothing he persisted: "Feel around behind the stomach." In exasperation the surgeon did—and his face underwent a startling change. He promptly turned to the patient with concentration again and this time he opened and drained an abscess which had developed entirely out of sight. When the patient awoke from the anesthetic, the pain was gone and the condition never returned.

While the word "precognition" sounds most formidable and certainly strange, it really isn't. Its strangeness fades quickly when you stop to think of it as a recognition beforehand that comes true. Remember how often people (whether someone you know personally or merely someone you learn about in the news media) experience this. Precognition is that familiar thing we call "premonition" which humanity has recognized and whose significance it has struggled with over hundreds of thousands of years—which has never quite been accepted fully and yet cannot quite be rejected.

Psychiatrists are very familiar with precognition, for their patients present them with such experiences in the course of therapy; it's the interpretation that makes the difference. One patient had a dream in which his attorney became ill and the very important lawsuit which was causing him so much anxiety had to be postponed. The buildup and tension would have to be repeated all over again at a later date. It did happen just as he'd dreamed it. One observer can see this as an unconscious wish coming true by coincidence. Another may interpret it as proof of precognition.

That mankind has long recognized some dreams as precognitive can be seen in 4,000-year-old Egyptian papyruses with their tales of dreams, in the Old Testament stories of Joseph's interpretations of Pharaoh's dreams or Daniel's of Nebuchadnezzar's. And in today's Brooklyn, at the famous Dream Laboratory of the Maimonides Medical Center Psychiatry Laboratory, Dr. Montague Ullman (a psychiatrist and psychoanalyst) and Dr. Stanley Krippner (a psychologist) have experimentally tested precognition in dreaming and found at least one sensitive who actually dreams precognitively, fourteen out of sixteen times. The dream scientists conclude that the likelihood of these results happening purely by chance would be something like a thousand to one.

In their research, Drs. Ullman and Krippner first looked for proof of telepathic transmission in sleep. While the subject slept in a soundproof room, the agent was in a distant room studying and trying to transmit images from special art prints, for example "Animals" by Tamayo in which two fierce dogs bare their fangs and tear at meat. The subject after dreaming (which can be recognized from eye movements, the so-called REM or rapid-eye-movement stage of sleep) was awakened and asked to relate the dream. Then investigators would decide whether the dream images coincided with the telepathic communication of the art print.

To test precognition, the subject was asked to predict which of the art prints would be selected next day by means of numbers chosen at random (a common statistical technique used in science and psychology). The psychic who hit fourteen out of sixteen in dreaming precognitively is an Englishman noted for predicting the time of de Gaulle's death, the wreck of an oil tanker (he "saw" time, national registration, and even ownership), and the date and result of the English elections.

From the standpoint of the practicing physician, precognition would certainly be a godsend to doctor and patient alike. My associate could have been spared major cranial surgery if a psychic had advised his doctor that the headache was a brain abscess which would only worsen unless antibiotics were given in time.

The proper psychic could warn of one danger which medicine is powerless today to predict or prevent, death from the anesthetic. Were we to know this in advance, different anesthetics could be used and the death rate in surgery reduced. Occult medicine could provide help and comfort for the doctor as well—as in the case of my patient who seemed to be dying but who was actually to return home in a few days. We would all have been spared a lot of torment if we had had experience enough with the psychics to realize we could believe them.

Parapsychologists have been working to prove precognition scientifically with those familiar Zener cards and by throwing dice. Volunteers are asked to predict in what order these cards will appear and after their prediction, the cards are mixed and then the accuracy of the precognition verified. With dice, the subjects attempt to predict the numbers that will come up and the dice are then rolled to check the prediction. But here, too, the proof of some people's ability to achieve significantly better scores than others (to have actual precognitive ability) is hotly debated. I feel the proof is there—in instances such as the seemingly dying patient I just mentioned, Dr. Ullman's English psychic, and the precognitive dreams humanity has always known and that witch doctors and priests have reported since the beginnings of recorded history. We simply do not yet know how to use it systematically.

Perhaps the most debatable of all the fields in the occult is psychokinesis—PK. This is the original mind-over-matter concept, tying in closely, some believe, with precognition and faith healing. PK is the name for Uri Geller's skill, which has taken so many people by storm and made many others suddenly sit up and take a new look at the occult. After all, it's pretty strong stuff when, without touching the objects, Uri uses mind power to bend a key to a 30° angle, twist a spoon almost like a pretzel, turn the hands of a wristwatch back more than an hour, and repair other watches merely by passing his hands over them. But there have been strong doubts raised about Geller and the validity of his demonstrations, as well as those of some of the other psychics also supposedly practicing PK on both sides of the Iron Curtain. *Time* (March 4, 1974) thoroughly explores Geller and some of the others and finds them distinctly suspect. For example, *Time* points out that Uri's PK capabilities have a very odd tendency to fade into nothingness or awkward excuses when magicians appear on the scene or air-tight checks against fraud are instituted: on the Johnny Carson *Tonight Show* for twenty minutes Geller failed repeatedly in his attempts at PK.

The argument has even recently spilled over into the British scientific journals. Obviously, if we could change physical things by mind power, operations and other such procedures could be performed with less trauma and more delicacy. In short, the potentialities would be limitless.

Some students of the occult feel that precognition is really a matter of PK—that the subject isn't really foreseeing what is going to happen but making what he sees come into being. Others feel that faith healing itself is also a matter of psychokinesis, the psychic producing actual physical changes to cure the disorder. J. B. Rhine and his group have recorded the attempts of subjects to make the numbers on dice come up as they wished but the results have been sharply questioned by many observers.

About PK, I'm open-minded and not convinced. Probably the most we can really say of PK today is that it's an exciting concept, that when it works—or seems to—it's a thrilling exhibition and a startling one. After all, Uri Geller did drive a car through traffic with a blindfold over his eyes. But then James Randi—who appears on TV strictly as an entertainer, "the Amazing Randi"—also drove through traffic, according to *Time*, with a mask and hood and pizza dough over his eyes. While Randi refuses to reveal his method, he emphasizes that there was no psi involved—it was just sheer deceit.

But what everyone asks is simply, "Are there *really* para-normal—psi—phenomena? Is ESP on the up and up?" Even those who believe wholeheartedly in parapsychology, ESP, and all the other aspects of the occult still recognize that there is a great deal of fraud and deceit being practiced in its name. For one thing, the process is so difficult to prove or disprove that it lends itself readily to abuses, to quacks and frauds who can exploit both the field itself and those naive followers who blindly accept virtually anything which calls itself the occult. However I feel that even many of the shabby practitioners really do possess ESP powers but act deceitfully when—as will invariably happen to anyone using emotional, psychological, or creative talents—they find themselves unable to perform well on demand. The greatest problem seems to be "tuning" the receiver, who, after all, has thousands of messages "in the air."

Before you're too hard on psychics, remember that physicians come out of a tradition of many thousands of years, that both society and their schooling try to imbue high values and standards in them, that they are licensed and therefore subject to special restraints—and yet Herbert S. Denenberg, Pennsylvania's nationally known consumer advocate and insurance commissioner, has found authoritative claims that anywhere from 5 to 15 percent of doctors are incompetent or dishonest. So one must look at the psychics and faith healers in perspective. For one thing, many are so committed to their work that the natural unevenness of all creative powers is disturbing to them and they just try too hard sometimes to prove their psychic ability and so find themselves either verging on the fraudulent or actively indulging in it.

Nevertheless, many knowledgeable and skeptical observers still feel—as I myself do—that there is a reality to these strange powers, that the psi phenomena *are* real and factual even though our understanding of them is shadowy and inadequate and we can only guess at the way it works. England's prestigious magazine *New Scientist* recently polled its scientific readership and found that almost three-quarters believed in at least the possibility of ESP. And Sigmund Freud—certainly one of the truly great scientific, medical, and psychological geniuses of all time—maintained an open mind toward the occult. He felt that telepathy might well be a real phenomenon and, if so, an exciting one filled with fascinating potential. He even thought it might well prove a common one as well. He called attention to the fact that children fear that their parents know their thoughts—a fear parallel to the adults' feelings about the omniscience of God—but he thought telepathy could well be the explanation in some cases, where the psychiatrist could find no other explanation for an incident.

True, all this leaves us with no positive answers—but then there isn't that much we know *absolutely* in any science. Everything we knew so positively in 1938 in medicine and science (in physics and chemistry for example) was pretty well shot down only ten years later and much had totally disappeared from the textbooks by 1958. After all, the most knowledgeable individuals would probably have laughed at the idea of antibiotics in the mid-thirties, or nuclear energy or trips to the moon as late as 1940. So Freud's open-mindedness is a good example from which all of us can learn.

There are some explanations for various of the psi phenomena, true. Some researchers in the occult talk of the universal energy which the psychic can tap or utilize. Others speak of God. The witches prefer to talk of gods (they have a nature religion with many deities). Some bring in electricity or thought waves or magnetism. I believe we will one day discover explanations for these phenomena which will satisfy the most "scientific." In the meantime, I personally think that love or the love-energy is the power in medicine that heals—and that miracles result from this enormous and extraordinary force.

7

Astrology: Moon, Murder, and Hemorrhaging

Let's look directly at the occult in medicine. How did astrology and the new moon figure in some 4,000 homicides in Florida and Ohio from 1956 to 1970? How do these same influences affect hemorrhaging after surgery—or the birth of children? Does witchcraft heal and how is acupuncture part of the occult? Can diseases be diagnosed by studying the palms of the hands—or by graphology? In short, is there a real medical use for the occult? Is the medical profession too conventional and tradition-bound to step outside the limitations of its current textbooks to utilize such new and esoteric procedures? Can surgery really be done without a knife by operating with the bare hands, producing neither blood nor scars nor wounds—or be performed on your "etheric" body without touching you at all?

In this chapter, I mean to view the range of those occult practices which may be of significant medical value to you. Here, too, you will see some of the reasons why I urge the use of holistic healing centers to provide a broad variety of possible diagnostic methods and treatment techniques for patient-help and the research necessary to determine scientifically and improve on the usable aspects of the medical occult. You may even learn in this chapter of sources of help for the future through conventional medical channels.

But always keep in mind that if you can get help from conventional and traditional medical care you *are* better off and the relief secured will be certain, safe, relatively simple, and not overly expensive (for a good psychic will charge you a fee in the same range as that of a competent physician—there's no saving money-wise). So I would urge you *first* to seek conventional medicine for any ailment. As we shall see later, there are times and conditions for which conventional help is the *only* answer, just as there are times when you should turn for help to occult medicine. Since this distinction is so important to your welfare, I'll set it aside for a detailed discussion in separate chapters.

Now, though, I'd like to explore occult medicine in its oldest and most elemental form, one that mankind has known since the dawn of time in this world of murder and madness, of hemor-rhages and childbirth and contraception, a world filled with strange and exciting possibilities. The old order doesn't always change, yielding place to new; ancient astrology is still with us, even in our daily speech. Take the word disaster (from the Italian *disastrato* or ill-starred); the word ill-starred itself; saturnine (of ob-vious connection with the planet Saturn); lunatic (from the Latin *lunaticus* or "moonstruck," crazy); and many others. And so we turn to what has been called the "Royal Art," astrology.

I'm really not sure myself whether astrology is an art or a science, because this basic distinction isn't nearly as clearcut and absolute as it's sometimes made to sound. All too often the distinc-tion lies more in the eye of the beholder than in reality and whether medicine or astrology is an "art" or a "science" is as much a matter of how they're being practiced as of any intrinsic quality.

To me, any field or discipline is an art if it utilizes intuition as a basic instrument, if it depends on subjective input. It's a science if it's all method and study and objectivity, if it can be performed well by anyone following the necessary formulas or techniques. It's like the cook who on hunch puts in a little of this and a bit of that, compared to the chemist who weighs his ingredients precisely to the millionth of a gram, all at exactly the correct temperature and humidity. Cooking is dependent on the individual cook while a chemical experiment can be accurately duplicated by anyone following the particular formula.

Astrology is called the "Royal Art" because when it was first developed as a special discipline—at least 5,000 years ago—it was intended for royalty or ruling families. Astrology was meant to provide these leaders with help—divinations of good or evil, indications of what they should or not do (when to attack in war, what the future would bring in the way of drought or crops, whom to appoint as prime minister). Astrology and astronomy were regarded as sister sciences and developed together. They were founded together before humanity had begun to record history.

Of all the occult practices, astrology is the most ancient and has always been the most revered. Closely tied to humanity's initial awareness of both itself and the world, it really started when people for the first time regarded the sun with wonder or stared into the sky at night to become aware of that bright large yellow globe and first noticed tiny pinpoints of light breaking the utter blackness overhead (for there was then neither pollution nor smog to dull their brightness). They must have very quickly noticed that the sun gave light and warmth; that some dots of light at night were brighter and some closer together or smaller; that others twinkled; and that the giant yellow globe varied in size and shape from night to night. As they improved their language and verbal communications and developed mathematics they learned to speak of "days" and "nights," and devised their first calendars.

But those strange bodies in the skies, so far away and so clearly beyond any human control, must early have taken on magical qualities. Ancient people depended on stars and the sun and the moon for their very life—to provide light which protected them from dangerous beasts by night, warmed them and made it easier for them to seek and find food, gave them light for whatever activities they desired. But sometimes those heavenly bodies seemed to disappear and people must have been terrified that they might not return.

Surely it took no great step to start worshipping the heavenly bodies, endowing them with mystical and magical powers, with awesome supernatural control over all the great uncontrollable events of life—the floods and the wild storms and the droughts that shaped the world. It took only a short step to ascribe to these mysterious objects an influence over personal destiny as well—success in battle or love, health and sickness. Turning these heavenly bodies into gods and demons gave people a certain measure of control over them for in this way they could be dealt with. One could bribe them with sacrifices or prayers, promise them rewards for their help, and study what they planned to do.

Astrology was in this way a "natural" science for it is eminently understandable how people began to look to these heavenly bodies, these beings in the heavens, seeking to understand them by their positions when a child was born or by mathematics or other charts people gradually devised. It was clear that these strange powers in the sky had been around as long as any people could recall—even the oldest—and as human records developed they showed that these distant stars and planets had seemingly always been there. People began to see the heavenly bodies as very personal, determining the pattern and the incidents of human life from birth to death. By the time of the classical Greeks and the early Egyptians, astrology had become a highly organized structure or system, in many ways difficult to distinguish from astronomy.

I believe astrology is a science of considerable value in medicine even though it has fallen into both disrepute and neglect.

However even the experts aren't that definite about astrology. The 1973 *Encyclopaedia Britannica* calls it an "art or science" while the completely new and radically altered 1974 edition of the same publication says astrology is "variously defined as a science or pseudoscience"; the 1970 *American Heritage Dictionary* defines it simply as a "study"; and the 1966 *Collier's Encyclopedia* terms it a "discipline."

It was only natural to believe that if astrology could foretell the future it could also predict the likely course and eventual outcome of an illness and even direct the treatment. This has proven one of the chief uses of astrology since before recorded history.

Astrology seems to satisfy something very deep in the human psyche for it appeared early and now—after a period of decline in the superscientific era of our recent past—it has suddenly experienced a healthy rebirth.

The Babylonians were avid astrologers and astronomers. The two studies evidently went hand in hand, with the likelihood that astrology came first. There's good evidence that the formal science of astrology was practiced in Babylonia, China, and Egypt far earlier than 6,000 years ago—and it may go back five or ten or twenty times that. The Babylonians believed that the sun, moon, stars, and planets were all gods and that a correct reading of the movements of these heavenly bodies could foretell earthly events.

So advanced were the Babylonian astrologers and astronomers that they were able to record accurately the rising and setting of the planet Venus more than 4,000 years ago.

Just as astrologers predicted the fortunes of the Babylonian royal family—in their wars and battles, their harvests and floods—so they tried to predict the course of any of their diseases and to prescribe treatment as well.

As we've already seen, astrology and medicine joined hands early. Mesopotamian astrologers looked for prophetic signs in the relationships of the heavenly bodies: the moon in particular foretold many things including the health of the king and his subjects. The early Greeks and Romans bickered a good deal over the medical value of astrology, but the great Hippocrates and later Galen both valued and used astrology.

The Greeks refined their astrology to a very high degree, giving control over particular parts of the body to the planets and to the signs of the zodiac: Cancer the Crab presided over the chest, Leo the Lion over the heart, and some body part was given to each of the other ten signs. The sun ruled the right side of the body and the heart, the moon the left side and the stomach, and so on for the planets.

A horoscope is cast for the time, date, year, and place of birth (today these figures are adjusted to Greenwich time for greater accuracy). This information makes it possible for the astrologer to draw up a chart showing the positions of the planets in the houses and in the signs of the zodiac at the time the person was born. This chart tells a great deal about the individual—although today's astrologer tends to look to the psychological rather than to the physical determinants. The early astrologers looked for indicators of ill-health and emphasized the individual's destiny, while today's practitioners look rather to the psychotherapeutic uses of this knowledge. By using the horoscope, the astrologer today may point out, for example, that there is undue hostility toward a parent or sibling, perhaps some feelings of inferiority, or difficulties arising from a broken home—all of which opens the way to deeper understanding of the self.

Contemporary astrology is very complicated, often involving Jungian or Adlerian psychology. But astrology always was a difficult and complex field whose mastery took long and arduous study. Without this knowledge, no physician was, at one time, considered really qualified to practice medicine. During the Middle Ages it was virtually unheard of for a doctor to question the authenticity of astrology. Astrologers had a status equal to that of physicians, and chairs of astrology were set up in many of the leading European universities. Our recent rational era led to the decline and near-disappearance of astrology which was suddenly out of fashion, something scientists sneered at.

But today! Just let your fingers wander through the "Yellow Pages," the classified telephone directory of your community, and you're likely to find a goodly collection of astrologers, astrological associations, and bookstores catering to this interest. Clearly, astrology is in the ascendance—planets, zodiacs, and all—and I think with good reason where medicine is concerned.

I sincerely believe that astrology can do a good deal to improve medical care. I feel we ought to bring this science back to the medical school, to the training of young doctors. True, astrology is far too complicated to be taught in its entirety as a part of medical school training, but it should be offered as a background course. Thus the doctor would at least know what astrology is and how it can be used, in a general sort of way. Later the medical practitioner can gain more knowledge about this science, as about any other specialty, through postgraduate continuing education. And computer programs would help in documenting astrological accuracy with all sorts of cross-correlations.

Before I explore in further detail the role of astrology in medicine, let me give you some indications here of how astrology might well be used. It would indicate the bad days for the surgical patient. Certain days are dangerous ones for each individual and lives might well be saved by avoiding surgery on the patient's bad days. Similarly, surgeons should not operate on their own bad days—they might better go fishing or play golf and leave the surgery to be performed by other surgeons on the staff. Perhaps in this way we might be able to lower mortality rates in surgery. Only recently for example, research was reported from the Biometeorological Research Center in Leiden, Holland. The researchers are said to have found that such things as blood pressure, hemoglobin, and sedimentation rate were affected by meteorological changes such as sunspots—this is evidence, if confirmed, of the influence of heavenly bodies upon mankind—astrology, if you will.

There is much hard evidence that astrology actually is involved in medicine in a strange linkage similar to the phases of the moon. People are still fascinated after hundreds of thousands or even millions of years of belief in the power of the moon. Yet in many ways it's still as much of a mystery as it was when people stood in an unconquered jungle or came out of their caves to gaze at this strange light in the sky, barely able to communicate their feelings and thoughts to each other.

For one thing, the moon on the horizon looks much larger than it does when directly overhead—and no one really knows why. There's a theory that we unconsciously correct visually for size when looking at distant things so that the object that's farther away will automatically seem larger to you. There's another possibility too—that we're so much more used to looking at the horizon than directly overhead that we make a larger correction automatically so that things we see on the horizon seem larger. And, there is one more explanation that some experts give—that the moon with a foreground of land or water produces a different mental scale and so seems larger. In short, that old devil moon still keeps its mystery and magic.

It's not surprising that the moon has always fascinated and impressed people with its power and influence. But it's also on occasion gotten a little more credit than it deserves. The "harvest moon" is actually only a full moon which rises some fifteen or twenty minutes later than usual (at the September equinox) and so gives farmers—supposedly but mistakenly—a little extra time for harvesting their crops. The full moon right after the harvest moon is called the "hunter's moon" although no one knows quite why.

But then there is still relatively little we do know about the moon and its influence on people, even though we've already walked its surface and studied its rocks and soil. Do we really howl during a full moon, are more babies born at that time, can the full moon really affect the mentally sick? We have some observations but only now do we have some hard facts. Of course, as a neurosurgeon I've spent a good deal of my professional life talking shop with others in my specialty and with neurologists; it's commonly acknowledged among my colleagues that during the full moon such problems as epileptic seizures and sleep-walking definitely do increase—although some tie this increase to any night with a bright moon (which could be either full or nearly full). And surgeons in general never cease to discuss which days are good or bad for operations, how the moon affects recovery or affects the operations themselves.

I grew up on a farm. In rural areas the phases of the moon, conception, and birth are commonly believed to be closely connected. There's an old belief that animals castrated during the full moon bleed to death. In fact, you will find physicians full of myths they've heard about bleeding—when it's likely to be worse and how it can be stopped or prevented. Only now we're going to see how some recent scientific studies have introduced hard data to prove that many of these myths about the moon may well be based on long centuries of shrewd folk observations of events whose simultaneous appearances finally led people to accept their relationship as cause-and-effect.

We know that the moon exerts gravitational forces which produce and affect the ocean tides, that these tide-generating forces also affect the solid body of the earth, and that even the very atmosphere has tides resulting from these same lunar gravitational forces. In 1971 a psychiatrist from the University of Miami School of Medicine, Dr. Arnold L. Lieber, presented a theory which I think is both imaginative and exciting—for it may well hold within it the reason for the moon's reputed effect on people, and perhaps also the key to the entire science of astrology.

Dr. Lieber suggests that the moon exerts its gravitational forces on the human body as well as on the earth—and produces regular changes in the water flow and balance in the body's tissues, which he calls the "biological tides." And the most exciting part of this is his evidence proving for the first time that the moon does influence human behavior. In a 1972 article in the *American Journal of Psychiatry* co-authored with Dr. Carolyn R. Sherin, also of his medical school, Dr. Lieber pointed out that if his lunar theory was correct, the greatest emotional changes should take place at the times of greatest bodily water movements, the "biological tides."

The team selected murder as an obvious and readily checked index of the amount of emotional disturbance. If the theory was correct, the times of strongest gravitational lunar pull (the new- and full-moon phases) should show an increase in homicides. Drs. Lieber and Sherin computerized the data on some 2,000 murders committed in Dade County, Fla., from 1956 to 1970, and a like number over almost the same period in Cuyahoga County, Ohio. The resulting graphs (plotting the numbers of homicides against the phases of the moon) look almost identical with sharp distinct peaks only at the full moon and the new moon phases.

There was also a difference qualitatively as well as quantitatively during these lunar phases. A study of the individual murders revealed that those committed during the new and full moons were of a particularly gruesome and savage nature as compared with those of other times. And, finally, there seems to be evidence that it's not just the murderers who were affected but everyone— for many of the crimes associated with the new or full moon seem to have been precipitated or brought on by the strange illogical actions of the victims themselves. I regard this scientific study as of crucial importance because for the first time it offers statistical objective proof that heavenly bodies (in this case the moon) can affect our health and behavior.

That all this makes me sound more like a medieval astrologer than a modern scientific neurosurgeon merely indicates that we are late in rediscovering and scientifically proving the reality of the truths behind our folk myths; new knowledge is opening in medicine. Perhaps we should give even more credence than we otherwise might to an article in the June 1, 1974, issue of *The National Observer* which reported interviews with a number of real live vampires, at least one of whom found her desire for vampirage really stimulated by the full moon. I'm always skeptical, but you can take the story or leave it as you see fit. Your guess is as good as mine because once you've read the report you'll know as much as I do about vampires and whether they even exist!

But, ignoring vampires, and coming back to the serious scientific aspects of astrology, let's look at the following relationship between lunar influences and hemorrhaging. A Tallahassee, Florida, nose and throat surgeon, Dr. Edson J. Andrews, has seen days in the operating room when there was virtually no bleeding while at other times hemorrhages were truly "the rule of the day." There isn't one of us in surgery who can't confirm this from our own experiences over the years.

In Tallahassee, one of Dr. Andrews' nurses pressed on him the concept that the moon was involved in bleeding. She even backed up her belief with a carefully kept record of his bleeders on a calendar—and they *did* come at the time of the full moon! In fact so distinct was this bunching of bleeding problems around the full moon that Dr. Andrews started a much more scientific and precise technique than the old one of circling dates on a calendar.

Fortunately Dr. Andrews approached this with the attitude of the true scientist. Much had been said, but nothing had ever been done to prove or disprove the myths; they had merely been discounted. Dr. Andrews gathered detailed records on all his tonsillectomies from 1956 through 1958, slightly more than a thousand. The "bleeders" were the patients who presented a problem in hemorrhage control—those who required special management during surgery, who had to be returned to surgery for hemorrhage control, or who needed special post-surgical medication to handle bleeding. The dates of these episodes were correlated with the phase of the moon: there is no mistake, the peak in the graphs—the greatest number of bleeders—is clearly at the full moon *with a startling* 82 *percent of all bleeders clustering around this time.*

Further emphasizing this increase in bleeding is the fact that there actually were fewer patients available around the full moon because reduced numbers were admitted at the very period when the number of bleeders was reaching its peak. Dr. Andrews also got confirmation from an Orlando physician who found this same pattern with his patients. The Tallahassee specialist found this pattern of increased hemorrhage repeating itself when he plotted the dates at which patients were admitted to his hospital for bleeding stomach ulcers.

Meanwhile Dr. Andrews, like any good scientist, moved further afield. Having heard that more babies were born at the full moon, he charted the births at Tallahassee Memorial Hospital for the period 1956 to 1958 and checked these, too, against the moon phases: 401 were born within two days of the full moon, 375 within two days of the new moon—and 320 within two days of the first quarter. He left it up to his readers to draw their own conclusions. He also calls attention to an English doctor who reports data proving that more natural deaths occur at the ebbing of the tide than at any other time (and tide results from the moon's gravitational forces).

Nat Freedland in *The Occult Explosion* reports that a Dr. Eugen Jonas of Czechoslovakia has an astrological birth control method which he believes has proven to be 99 percent effective. By determining the correct astrological time for intercourse, the Czech doctor can predict the sex of the baby with 95 percent accuracy. He supposedly is 87 percent right in foretelling the coming child's sex once he knows the time of impregnation. And birth defects, Jonas believes, are due to conception under the wrong planetary influences. He found, for example, that one woman who had given birth only to stillborn children could safely conceive only four days in the year. Using his information she was finally able to have a normal child. As an old farmer, I find the notion that moon phases have a role in conception or birth a familiar one. Dr. Jonas' ideas seem possible to me and I look forward to further proof when the tests being carried out elsewhere in Europe are completed.

I must confess that astrology seems to me an exciting and fertile field for medical research. Strip conventional medicine of its preconceptions and prejudices, and we may be on the verge of a whole series of breakthroughs not the least of which are likely to be in astrology where scientific evidence is finally accumulating. Growing numbers of doctors are recognizing this as they—like Drs. Lieber and Edson—turn to these neglected fields. One East Coast surgeon I know has a private astrologer whom he uses to provide insights into his patients' personalities so that he can offer better medical care and handling.

A Northeastern physician is very much interested in using astrology to determine in advance which parents are likely to have retarded and which to have gifted children. One doctor seeks to use this ancient science to tell whether an unborn infant will have emotional disorders so that very early help can be provided.

I'm certain that out of this ferment will come a whole range of positive helping roles for astrology in medicine. Clearly, those physicians who lived in what we once so arrogantly and mistakenly termed "The Dark Ages" knew a great deal more than we have given them credit for over these last few centuries. Perhaps even the tens of millions who today follow their horoscopes daily in the newspapers really do have good reason for it. However, I agree that there is too much misinformation and downright fakery—too little real science—in much popular astrology.

Witches, Etheric Surgery, Palmistry, and Graphology

It's often said that you can't live in America and not know at least one witch. But if you know more than one, they'll likely disagree even about what witchcraft itself is! To most people it's simply an ancient nature religion, while to others it's Satanism or black magic. My own knowledge of witchcraft is, frankly, limited. Courses are being given in it everywhere today. All sorts of rituals are reported in newspapers, magazines, and books.

According to *The New York Times*, a Kansas warlock (a male witch) has won reinstatment in his civil service job as a psychologist—with back pay—because it was discriminatory to fire him for practicing his religion. The news media carry a steady stream of stories about voodoo slayings, strange rituals, and voodoo colonies in the United States. There was even a convention of magicians, warlocks, and witches recently in the very heartland of America, in Minneapolis, close to my own La Crosse.

We recently interviewed a witch, and one of the more knowl-edgeable ones. He is young, handsome, tall and blond (as un-witch-like as one can imagine), a free-lance writer now working on a book about his craft, particularly in Greater New York, where he knows of sixteen different witch sects (not one of which worships the devil). How many witches are there in America? Well, this witch knows of one sect alone which has some 150,000 members and a sect of foreign witches out in Nebraska. But there is a counterreaction: *The New York Times* recently reported a planned tour by a "Witchmobile," an anti-occult mobile unit with which an evangelist hoped to inform the country's teenagers about such things as the black mass, blood-drinking orgies (whose reality I certainly question), voodoo oils, and the like.

The craft (which is how witches refer to their religion) isn't new of course for there are horned creatures carved into rocks all across Europe from the Soviet Union (which is said to have a lib-eral supply of its own witches) to Spain—and some of these figures go back more than 30,000 years. Witchcraft—pagan or nature religion is really what it is—was certainly begun the first time peo-ple thought of religion or of a supernatural power structure, and this must go back to our very beginnings. And whether you call them white witches or just plain witches, they feel they can be channels for that universal energy (love?) which is available and can be focused for healing.

In short, witches too can heal, but when they talk of this they seem no different from any other faith healers. *I personally feel that when a witch heals, he or she does it by his or her clairvoyant abilities, not witchcraft.* Sudden popular interest has too often brought faddists and quacks and given witchcraft a bad name. I re-spect the craft as a serious ethical religion, but my expertise is in medicine and I can speak authoritatively only about the healing aspects of witchcraft. I see no difference in their healing powers from those of any other psychic or faith healer.

There is one far-out occult technique that merits mention if only as a warning, for its patterns are distinctly suspicious, even to faith healers. Seattle has become the staging area, the jumping-off place, for a twentieth-century American crusade. Filled with the same blind faith that recruited the iron-clad medieval warriors, these people (some thousand of them in 1973) gather in groups and travel far across the Pacific to Manila in search of their individual Holy Grail, their own health and cure. For these are people who either believe or have been told that modern medicine can do nothing for them. Waiting for them in the Philippines are magic psychic or etheric surgeons who perform operations, usually with little or no bleeding or pain or discomfort—and virtually always without leaving any scar or other aftereffects.

The United States Federal Trade Commission has now gone to court to protect these desperate and gullible people.

Take Mr. and Mrs. D of Seattle. Mrs. D, still a young woman, discovered a lump on her neck and recalled her breast surgery for cancer more than five years before. Her doctor confirmed her dread—the old cancer had returned and the prognosis was hopeless, a year or two perhaps. The Ds listened to the blandishments of a travel agency which promised miraculous cures without pain or scarring. In desperation, along with some thousand others, the Ds left for Manila and psychic surgery. But Mr. D, more cynical, seized the tissue the etheric surgeon had supposedly removed from Mrs. D and popped it into a bottle of preservative for later analysis by experts back in the United States. When this tissue was analyzed by American experts it proved to be a piece of animal bowel.

No doctor interested in his or her patients' welfare wants to debunk anything that may make them feel better but psychic surgery can accomplish this only psychologically, temporarily, and at an absurd and terrible price. The use of etheric surgery has often led to the discontinuance of regular treatment. The *Journal of the American Medical Association* (*JAMA*) recently reported that one eight-year-old boy with bone cancer was taken for etheric surgery and his conventional anticancer therapy stopped during the trip. He returned with an arm so badly swollen that it had to be amputated and he died shortly. Time after time the tissue "removed" by etheric surgery has proven to be the same old fraud—animal tissues or fat.

But let's see how this "surgery" is done. Magicians have shown repeatedly that these "operations" can be faked and I might add a strictly medical note here. I've seen movies of the famed Philippine psychic surgeons and there is no question in my mind that they do *not* enter the body. You must understand that you can push your whole fist down into the abdomen of a reclining relaxed person; pictures taken in profile will then make it look as if you're actually putting your hand directly into the abdomen even though all you're doing is indenting the unbroken skin. There is no doubt in my mind that this "surgery" is not surgery.

However, I do feel that these psychic surgeons may conceivably on occasion accomplish the same thing that the faith healer does. *JAMA* interviewed a clinical psychologist from the Seattle area who agrees with this. I recently lectured on psychic diagnosis in England and spoke with a famous British anthropologist who also feels that on rare occasions some people undergoing etheric surgery may be helped—not by the surgery but by whatever *magic* it is that makes faith healing work, what makes sugar pills so consistently effective, *the same magic a mother works when she kisses her hurt child.* It's the same magic performed by the doctor or nurse who pats a patient's arm, offering the little reassurance that *does* perform miracles.

What psychic surgery does accomplish can be done with far less damage by standard faith healing. Some pay dearly for neglecting their medication, other hopeless patients suffer a terrible letdown when after the cruel buildup this last hope proves to be just a hoax. Besides the loss of money, the sufferers are often considerably damaged by the effects of the long trip in their weakened state.

But not far from the leading center for this fakery is the home of a much more useful occult tool. For just across the South China Sea from the Philippines is the land where acupuncture was born. Exactly how acupuncture works is still a hotly argued question. In any case, acupuncture really was born—originally—out of the occult as you can see just by looking at the reasons its Chinese originators give for the way it works.

Acupuncture was first mentioned in a Chinese commentary of some 2,500 years ago (as was the method of diagnosing illnesses by taking the pulse). The beliefs that led to acupuncture are complex and, frankly, not entirely clear to me (or anyone else so far as I can determine). Involved are cosmology and magic, along with *Yin* and *Yang* (Yin being cold, dark, female, negative; and Yang warm, light, male, positive). The Chinese, you see, were clearly male chauvinists.

It is, according to the Chinese, the balance of Yin and Yang—their harmony—that determines health or illness. The body is considered a sort of miniature cosmos, with philosophy and politics also involved and the body politic compared to the human body. The more you study this system, the more complicated it seems to become.

In my view, we have to see acupuncture as two wholly different treatment modalities even though the needles and points are the same. For the treatment of disease, this strange (to Westerners) gibberish of Yin and Yang, of humors and elements has, I believe, no scientific basis and acupuncture is almost worthless for most disease. *But* there is another world of acupuncture—the world of pain—and here acupuncture is amazingly effective and I've used it with good results for years. But I believe the real reasons are physiological. This is too complex to explore here so I'll ask you to bear with me until we discuss pain and my recommendations as to when you should turn to the occult for help with pain.

Another ancient practice is a simple old-fashioned word we have all seen on store windows emblazoned with a palm with mystic markings, lines, and crosses. Inside, an old gypsy woman—or a young one perhaps—would be ready to unfold the secrets of your past, present, and future, all from the lines on your palms. It's probably more than 6,000 years old. Practiced in China, most likely from the earliest days, it's still widely performed in India where the gypsies originated and probably learned the craft of chiromancy—another name for palmistry.

It all looked like sheer nonsense—and was regarded as such except for the famous British scientist Sir Francis Galton who, in 1890, proved the value and dependability of fingerprints for identification (whether of the infant in the hospital or the criminal seeking to escape justice). I myself have only recently found the palmist of use along with other psychics and practitioners of the occult in making medical diagnoses (a palmist was in that group of psychics I tested out scientifically at my clinic in La Crosse).

Palmistry or chiromancy, over many thousands of years, has developed detailed explanations of virtually all the ridges and forked lines, the creases and grooves, the mounds, and the rest of the palm's features. Palmistry is truly a universal art that has been practiced by the people of every country, every place and time. The Old Testament itself is cited as an authority by the palmists, who interpret any of its remarks about hands as giving the weight of the Bible to palmistry.

The nomenclature of chiromancy was developed in ancient Rome and Greece and it's still used: the mound on your palm at the base of the wrist is Luna, the mount (mountain) of the Moon (this shows moral character, sensitivity and so on); at the base of the pinkie and third finger is the mount of Mercury (the love of knowledge, science, industry and the like); and so it goes. The hand has been mapped out with a detailed, formalized plan which permits a virtually mechanical and unthinking interpretation. The lines of the palm indicate intelligence, length of life, good forture, health, et cetera.

First palmistry was a religious practice employed by witch doctors, medicine men, and priests. Then for many centuries in Europe, palmistry was deeply respected by thinking and learned people as well as by the multitude. It was taught in the universities, the centers of learning. Then it became a way for itinerant gypsies to earn a precarious living at county fairs or on the backstreets of the big cities.

But along with the rest of the occult, palmistry today has gained both popular and serious followers. I felt I should include a palmist when testing practitioners of the occult—and the palmist proved about as good as the others, except for the clairvoyants, as you shall see later. Here too the ancient lore of mankind stands up, for palmistry—with its assertion that from the skin of the palm one can tell much about the human being's life, health, and psychological traits—offers a good deal to medicine.

Science has only recently discovered and proven that these complex patterns found on the palms of the hands and the soles of the feet and the undersurfaces of the tails of some monkeys are valuable in diagnosing medical problems. But now it's called "dermatoglyphics" (skin carvings)—a new scientific name for that old palmistry which the ancient witch doctors practiced universally when humanity was still young.

Actually, skin patterns—fingerprints and the like—are formed about the twelfth week after conception. While these undulations and structures grow in size, the basic pattern never changes; fingerprints can remain the same for nearly a century and are so individual that even those of identical twins are different. And those of a more than 2,000-year-old Egyptian mummy are still clearly visible. Fingerprints and palm prints are medically helpful for they are virtually diagnostic in mongolism (Down's syndrome, congenital idiocy), or where the mother has suffered rubella or German measles during her pregnancy and the fetus has been affected. There is even some talk of diagnosing other disorders such as schizophrenia but this is still a new and relatively unexplored field. In any case there may be much more to palmistry than we ever thought—and certainly the palmist achieved a reasonable success in diagnosing my patients.

Close to palmistry is graphology. Obviously this can't go back as far as other aspects of the occult, for handwriting that could be examined by this method only goes back some 3,000 or 4,000 years. (But perhaps the Egyptians had their own graphologists to interpret the way they drew their hieroglyphics!) In any case, graphology—the study of handwriting particularly with reference to the character of the writer—certainly goes back 2,000 years. For even that long ago there were comments made on the handwriting of Octavius Augustus. The Chinese were interested in the relationship between handwriting and personality 1,000 years ago.

The graphologist looks for such clues as the size of the letters, the spaces between the letters, and the way these are formed. Is the stroke smooth and even or one with jerky movements or uneven pressure? Are there breaks or disruptions in what should be a smooth stroke? How fast is the writing, do the letters slope, is the thickness uniform or uneven, are connections smooth and even, are there any sharp angles?

Graphology is really the examination of physiological and neurological functioning. To write, your brain and nerves and muscles, your hand, and all its parts are involved. Any neuromuscular changes in the body will produce a change in your handwriting. In fact there have been many claims that handwriting actually reveals both the physical and the psychological health of the writer. One of Asia's leading psychiatrists regards graphology as "an acceptable component of modern psychology." For your handwriting is probably as individual and unique as your palm or your fingerprints or your face, and a well-trained graphologist can come up with an amazing amount of information from your handwriting. It's only one facet of a psychological examination, but our largest corporations are said to use graphologists to assess their employees.

Some graphologists claim they can diagnose health problems from handwriting and even spot specific diseases. This is a specialty called grapho-diagnostics and one expert—Chicago's well-known Alexandria East—says it's not unusual for handwriting to reveal such medical conditions as blood disorders, slipped disc, hardening of the arteries, and drug problems. Ms. East tells of a Midwest executive who discovered that his signature was being forged. The graphologist he hired detected hemorrhoids as one of the physical problems of the man doing the forging. Only one man working there had this medical problem and—confronted with this fact—he confessed!

Clearly, graphology is another ancient technique based on real observation—but my own feeling is that many of the graphologists actually are clairvoyants who use their psychic powers in addition to scientific measurements.

The Dangers
in Conventional
Medicine

Drugs, Tests,
and X-rays

Your physician today has powerful medications effective
against conditions as different as venereal disease and cancer. But all too often, instead of being saviors, doctors
have become drug pushers, the worst offenders, as a
group, in addicting people to everything from narcotics to
tranquilizers. To many of the more responsible and concerned members of my own profession the figures are
enough to make the hackles rise. The result of overuse of
antibiotics may well be the loss of medical control over
such diseases as typhoid fever—a return to the 1930s when
doctors stood by helplessly and watched 10 to 15 percent of
these patients die, while other unfortunate victims of this
terribly debilitating disease suffered through weeks of infection and slow convalescence. Vastly increasing numbers of
patients are also being sent to the hospital with adverse reactions to drugs often given improperly or promiscuously.
Deaths from these adverse drug reactions are running to

tens of thousands a year and increasing annually while the cost of hospitalizations due to these same reactions runs to $3 billion a year.

Harried, severely pressured, overworked, haunted by the decisions of life and death they must make so often, and constantly propagandized by the drug houses, doctors today suffer serious emotional problems. Narcotics addiction, alcoholism, suicide, and marital difficulties have become occupational hazards of the practice of medicine. The incidence of narcotics addiction among doctors is from thirty to a hundred times that reported for the population as a whole. The most recent figures I've seen indicate that 400 or more doctors are lost to practice annually as a result of alcoholism, another 200 or more from narcotics addiction, and yet another 100 by suicide. Broken marriages have been shown to be tragically common among physicians.

Diagnostic tests, like drugs, are also often overused, again for unhealthy emotional reasons. These are usually done *not* for malicious or stupid reasons but out of a haunting fear of missing something and a fear of malpractice suits. In my field alone, neurosurgery, I would guess that probably well over 500,000 special brain and spinal cord studies (such as injecting air or special solutions for X-rays) are done annually and out of these 5,000 patients are likely to suffer significant complications. Some tests can precipitate or even produce a stroke. Yet only about one in ten of these tests ever reveals a problem which can be helped surgically. The other 90 percent are performed unnecessarily and at least 70 percent of the time without any really serious medical reason.

These are some of the problems of conventional medicine— but to condemn all conventional medicine for these shortcomings would be simply throwing out the baby with the bathwater. You must learn the details, understand, and evaluate, to protect yourself and to become a wiser patient.

It was to circumvent many of these shortcomings that I turned to the occult, to alternative approaches to medicine. But there is no perfect answer to any problem; there is no panacea either in medical practice or in life itself. (Chapter 11 will probe this question of when to use conventional or traditional medicine and when to turn to occult medicine.)

A good many physicians today—and I am one—feel that the medical profession must bear a sizeable part of the blame for the current addiction problem in our nation. Certainly every one of us who has worked with chronic pain patients can recite a long list of patients who have come for help, already severely addicted by their doctors who kept giving stronger and ever stronger narcotics instead of turning to specialists for consultation and help when the patient's pain failed to respond. I think virtually every chronic pain patient who comes to the pain clinic for help is addicted—and I'm certain there are many more patients who never seek this special help and may not even know it exists.

Patients show up at headache clinics with shoeboxes filled with narcotics. At my pain clinic I've seen patients with skin like elephant hide from repeated injections of narcotics and others with hat boxes, attaché cases, and kits of all kinds chock-full of painkilling drugs of every strength, kind, and description. Tranquilizers and sedatives, too, are favorites for these poor sufferers who then become habituated, either physically or psychologically, to these drugs as well.

Let's just take a look at the figures. In 1970 the drug industry turned out 5 billion doses of tranquilizers, another 5 billion of barbiturates, and 3 billion of amphetamines (what's known to our drug culture as "speed"). That same year over 2 billion prescriptions were given out by physicians—and some 350 million of these were for mood-altering drugs (tranquilizers, sedatives, and the like). In fact, a careful study by Dr. Paul D. Stolley, professor of medicine at The Johns Hopkins Medical School, showed that the drugs most prescribed by doctors were the psychoactive ones, the mood-altering medications.

Oddly, the medical profession itself is well aware of this overdosage, for a recent survey by Harvard's Dr. David C. Lewis showed that two-thirds of the physicians questioned admitted they felt that doctors were overprescribing the psychoactive drugs. Yet the recklessness continues. All of this, I feel, is due to a combination of factors. For one thing, drug houses are spending $750 million a year on physicians—$2,500 a year *per doctor*—to push their products with giveaways of all kinds, complimentary supplies of drugs, detail men to dance attendance on doctors in their offices and at their meetings (where drug houses often supply free food and drink and whatever). So outrageous has this influence become that the U.S. Department of Health, Education and Welfare now favors strict limitations on such practices. The staff of the Senate Health Subcommittee, chaired by Senator Edward M. Kennedy, found that twenty major drug companies spent $14 million on gifts for health professionals and gave away 2 billion free samples of drugs last year.

But the other cause of overprescribing lies in the very nature of the patients' complaints. I've mentioned that 85 percent of the patients seen by doctors have psychosomatic complaints. Look at some of the statistics: of 200 patients admitted to a general hospital for surgery, 86 percent had emotional problems; of 1,000 patients of an internist (a specialized form of general practitioner who deals with a cross-section of medical problems), 72 percent had *purely* psychosomatic disorders and the rest had a large psychosomatic component; and, finally, of almost 300 patients admitted to a medical ward in one of our largest cities, 67 percent suffered diagnosable psychiatric disorders.

At least a million and a half patients enter hospitals every year suffering adverse drug reactions. A recent federal report estimates the cost at some $3 billion. Both figures are likely to be very much higher by the time you read this. Tens of thousands of patients die of adverse drug reactions and Senator Kennedy, opening the hearings of his Health Subcommittee, suggested that the actual death toll may well be as high as 140,000 a year—with 80 percent of these preventable! Some studies indicate that these adverse reactions occur in from a tenth to a third of all hospital patients. There is no way of determining how many occur in physicians' private offices where fear of malpractice suits alone would materially reduce the number either admitted or reported or even recorded.

Even the "miracle drugs" are proving somewhat less than truly miraculous, for they can and do kill. There are cases on record where patients have died because a simple uncomplicated cold was treated with a prescribed antibiotic which the doctor should have known to be deadly. (The common cold cannot be treated with any medication known to man today: you just have to rest, drink fluids, take vitamin C, perhaps take an aspirin for any aches or fever—and wait.) The antibiotics are the worst offenders when it comes to adverse drug reactions—yet physicians, ignoring or ignorant of these facts, still turn to these "miracle drugs" much too often.

When we realize that 85 percent of the diseases a doctor sees are psychosomatic, it's obvious that most patients should not be treated with drugs but with something which is as nonphysical as the complaint itself. And here is where the occult—and the faith healer or the psychic—can be so useful, since medicine's weakest point is the treatment of the psychosomatic disorder. The medical student is never actually taught how to deal with psychosomatic disorders (although some schools do call attention to the fact that psychotherapy is indicated) even though they're going to be the chief problem in practice. I'm not even sure that medicine knows *how* to deal with this problem—so why not give the faith healers a crack at it? I personally suspect that a good percentage of faith healings are psychosomatic. It seems to me that this is a perfect area for the faith healers; they can do no harm here, only good.

There's a tendency, in the excitement of the many achievements of modern medicine, to forget that the same tests which serve us so well can also be dangerous and even deadly, that many of our sophisticated medical procedures carry a distinct element of risk with them, that they are there to be used wisely but sparingly—to be considered carefully, not rushed into routinely. And in the hospitals where most tests are performed, the life-saving measure is found side by side with the life-threatening. Hospitals are alarmingly vulnerable to infections which we once thought were conquered and on the verge of disappearing.

Because many of our diagnostic tests are actually dangerous as well as diagnostic, I would hate to use them in a borderline situation—as in my own wife's case. In cerebral arteriograms (the injection of special dense "contrast" materials into the chief neck and head arteries which supply the brain, to make these vessels show up clearly on X-rays) there is one chance in 200 of causing a stroke. The devastation of this outcome outweighs the fact that the risk is small and makes me feel that cerebral arteriograms are to be avoided wherever possible. There is the pneumoencephalogram, in which brain fluid is removed and replaced by an injection of air into certain spaces of the brain to outline its parts for X-ray. Such tests and examinations should not be undertaken lightly, so far as I'm concerned.

My particular interest in these neurological tests obviously stems from the fact that neurosurgery is *my* specialty—or, rather, was for so long. In this field I can speak with the extra knowledge of the specialist when I say that fewer than one in three of these contrast procedures for X-rays actually reveals any physical abnormality. There are some 2,500 neurosurgeons in the United States and on the average they do 300 to 500 or more of these diagnostic procedures a year. Then there are the contrast injections for spinal X-rays; all together these contrast tests are probably carried out at least three-quarters of a million times a year. Yet two-thirds of these never show any physical abnormality. Certainly not more than 10 or 15 percent reveal a surgically correctable or even treatable physical abnormality. Most of these tests are done because the doctor feels a minimal suspicion—and one in 200 of the patients (some 7,500 all told) suffer serious complications.

When you realize that all this is in a single medical specialty, you can guess what must be going on in general practice and all the other medical specialties. For example, a close relative of mine had a fertility problem and saw an East Coast gynecologist. In his examination he blew a hole in her Fallopian tube; she developed peritonitis and nearly died. This sort of practice is extremely common, unfortunately.

So it seems to me that when doctors have only a suspicion and no real concrete reason to do one of these treacherous tests, when there is no good reason to think that something definite will be revealed and that the problem can be cured once it is located, they should seriously consider first asking a couple of good psychics: "Does this patient need this? Should I risk this examination?"

Many tests require hospitalization but the danger of this is that hospitals themselves are increasingly plagued by the worst communicable disease problem that America now faces—one which may be costing us as much as $20 billion a year in medical and other expenses such as lost income and all the other incidentals that go into the costs of major and often fatal illnesses. Nobody knows what the figures really are, but I've heard estimates varying from $50 million on up into the billions—and estimates of the frequency of hospital-spread infections vary almost as widely, with figures from 2 percent to 15 percent being mentioned. Mortality rates, too, are vague and hard to pin down, with estimates ranging from the tens of thousands to a hundred thousand or more. One hospital outbreak was traced to an anesthetist's fingernail—it produced nearly 200 cases of pneumonia. In Sweden, 200 patients are said to have come down with dysentery from salmonella-contaminated thyroid pills imported from the United States. America itself has suffered infections resulting from contaminated intravenous fluids used in hospitals. And so the stories go.

Another area of growing concern to knowledgeable physicians today is the X-ray. From April through September 1970, for instance, there were 180 million X-rays taken in the United States. That's a lot of X-rays, a lot of people exposed to potentially deadly radiation. Many experts are deeply concerned over the thousands of cancers of all types that may be produced by this radiation. As many as 30,000 lives a year may be lost as a result of excessive X-rays, but most experts discount this figure as too high.

Certainly radiology is an example of the overuse of a valuable tool for which there is almost no substitute. Most radiologists are disturbed by the dangerous overuse of X-rays. Dr. Alexander R. Margulis, chairman of the Department of Radiology of the University of California in San Francisco, reports a study in which fifty-five skull X-rays showed only one with anything wrong. Another study reveals that one-fifth of skull X-rays are taken for very minor injuries and more than a third are taken only to avoid any possible liability in case of malpractice suits.

The concern here, of course, is whether we are causing cancer, with the risk directly proportional to the numbers of X-rays taken. Again, I feel that a good psychic diagnostician can relax the doctor, calm his or her fears, and thus reduce the vast number of unnecessary X-rays. One boy, by the time he was thirteen, had had more than seventy-six X-rays of his spine for a congenital condition (one present at birth) which was actually causing no problem.

There is a clear thread running through all of this—the concern of the doctor that he or she might fail to treat the patient sufficiently, might miss the infection, might not spot some bony defect or condition. The physician is haunted by a fear of not doing enough for the patient—but in reality there is usually little reason to fear that the doctor will miss that vital something, that key fact. The most prevalent problem in American medicine today is not undertreatment but overtreatment with all its pitfalls.

What the doctor really needs—and therefore the patient as well—is some other *safe* way of being reassured about the diagnosis, something on which the doctor can fall back to confirm the decision that the psychoactive drug, the antibiotic, the complex dangerous test, or the extra X-ray is unnecessary. And this is where, I feel, the occult practitioner—what I would like to call the psychic physician's assistant or the psychic diagnostician—would be so valuable. He or she could relieve the doctor's anxieties and uncertainties by confirming clinical judgments so that care can be administered with only the necessary procedures. The doctor would not feel compelled to do something "just to be on the safe side." Harry had a fever and the doctor prescribed antibiotics— risking an adverse reaction—for fear the diagnosis *might* be wrong. The doctor suspected that Harry might have a bacterial infection instead of the flu (which is caused by a virus). Antibiotics are useless against a virus, but the doctor wanted to be on the safe side.

10

American Surgery: Use, Abuse, and Overuse

I'm a surgeon and I must confess to ambivalent feelings about my specialty, a mixture of pride and shame. For American surgery today can be justly proud of its brilliant achievements, its awe-inspiring record of pushing back the grasp of death itself—and this is shown most clearly and dramatically in surgical transplants. A kidney transplant has now been in place and is still operating perfectly after nearly twenty years while the heart transplanted into a Midwest junior high school teacher has reached its sixth anniversary.* Entire hips and now whole knees are being replaced for sufferers who could not walk before. Heart conditions are relieved by implanting new blood vessels on the surface of the heart. Open-heart surgery is common, and surgery is still the surest hope for most forms of cancer.

* Louis B. Russell, Jr., of Indianapolis, died in late November 1974, having survived six years, three months, and three days with a "borrowed" heart.

I could go on naming the miracles of surgery almost indefinitely—but there is also a seamy side to American surgery, one which has turned it at times into a tragedy of overuse and abuse. Misuse of operations has produced accusations of "knife-happy surgeons"—charges which are unfortunately well-founded. For while surgery has relieved suffering and extended both the period and the quality of life with one hand, it has threatened all this with the other. Unfortunately there is always a certain risk in surgery and the death rate commonly runs between 1 and 2 percent (rarely if ever below 0.5 percent); results too are not always what we would like them to be.

Then too there are fads in surgery just as in society itself. I've seen operations become popular and sweep the profession as wildly and thoughtlessly as the bobby-sox craze or raccoon coats or long hair or jeans swept the country itself. In surgery the current rage at any particular time may be appendectomies or hysterectomies or tonsillectomies (once done as a matter of routine)—but it can even go so far as using an icepick to perform massive crippling brain surgery or performing operations on the spine for conditions that don't even exist. I've seen too much of this—and talked about it. As a result, young people often ask me how it comes about.

Most often, the immediate fashion in surgery is the result of a particular time or place, a new idea or theory or procedure that suddenly looks good and catches on. In these circumstances, it is simply a matter of surgeons being human. And only time and proof can change or end any craze—for medical or surgical fads usually die away as the proof seeps in and the picture no longer has the heady exciting rosy glow it had when it was new and incompletely understood.

But sometimes there is more than faddism at work—for one can hear in the locker rooms of hospitals remarks about "acute remunerative appendicitis," or "when in doubt cut it out," or that gimmicky comment which has descended through generations of surgeons: "Everybody has at least three surgical diseases—all you have to do is find them." But there is also the warning that isn't listened to sufficiently: "You can't cut out pain with a knife." And it was this failure to heed the old warning that almost drove me to quit neurosurgery right at the start.

This is a strange half-world of medicine, an area where the surgeon or physician (nonsurgeons have often performed these radical procedures) forgets the sacred Hippocratic oath and ignores its pledge to do no harm. For in psychosurgery, deliberate damage and destruction is visited on that most sacred, most personal, and most vitally human part of the human being—the mind.

In 1936 Dr. Antonio de Egas Moniz, a Portugese neurologist, performed the first lobotomy. Actually he is said to have completed only some twenty of these monstrous operations before the Portuguese government outlawed the procedure, for purely political reasons. Moniz was awarded the Nobel prize in 1949 for his work in devising this operation. The method had been suggested before tranquilizers and antipsychotic drugs were available for the very sickest mental patients. At that time, nearly forty years ago, there was some reason for this operation, called variously (it has many different types and modifications) a frontal lobotomy, a cingulotomy, a leucotomy, or a tractotomy.

Basically these all add up to the same thing—destruction of essential parts of the brain to produce a quieter, calmer, more manageable person—one with marked personality changes. In short, someone who was less troublesome to those around him—but a person who was now just that much less human: less able to feel or judge, less sensitive and aware of himself, and with less empathy and capacity for love.

Within a few months of Moniz' first such operation, Dr. Walter S. Freeman, an American neurological surgeon, began to do lobotomies at St. Elizabeth's Hospital in Washington, D.C. The operation quickly caught on and the pace at which it was being done picked up rapidly. Many of the early ones were simply done in doctors' private offices, even by nonsurgeons, so elementary is the actual procedure of destroying a part of the brain. Increasingly lobotomies attracted interest and Dr. Peter R. Breggin, a psychiatrist on the faculty of the Washington (D.C.) School of Psychiatry, has said that the first wave of lobotomy and psychosurgery (the terms are often used synonymously, although psychosurgery is that surgery performed on the psyche or mind) through the 1950s involved some 50,000 patients in the United States and about a third that number in Great Britain.

But with the introduction of the psychoactive drugs in the early 1950s, psychosurgery began to decline. The powerful new medications (special potent tranquilizers are very effective with psychotics, the severely mentally ill) calmed and controlled the patients. Unfortunately there recently seems to be a revival of all this soul-surgery (for the psyche or mind really *is* the soul). The story is not pleasant. Dr. Breggin shocked and informed the nation by inserting into the *Congressional Record* of February 24, 1972, the story of the extent to which this surgery is still being carried on. Children under the age of eleven and even under five are being lobotomized by burning or the injection of olive oil into their brains. Ultrasonic energy and electrodes are being used to destroy brain tissue instead of just cutting it apart. Dr. Breggin finds evidence of up to 600 lobotomies now being performed every year in the United States and concludes that "well over 100,000 persons have already been subjected to psychosurgery around the world."

I myself turned toward controlling pain through nondestructive methods and so found my own niche in neurosurgery. The only times I have ever even considered psychosurgery for my patients has been where the case is hopeless (usually terminal cancer) and no other hope seemed available for controlling the torture. However, these operations are rarely successful in the long run. My new electrical techniques offer far more help than these destructive surgical techniques.

The effect of psychosurgery hasn't been too good even for the medical profession itself. My associate was told that there are many guilt feelings left over in the medical profession from those early days of indiscriminate lobotomies. One doctor told Dr. Breggin that he himself had performed nearly 5,000 of these operations. Dr. Breggin's own strongly antipsychosurgery stand has now found considerable support in our profession.

But this is not the only problem with American surgery. In

many ways surgery itself has become a wasteland instead of a creative, productive field. Repeatedly the question is asked both by the public and the medical profession: "Is there just too much surgery?"

I can only answer "YES!" From 20 to 60 percent of all operations performed (some 14 to 20 million a year in the United States) are unnecessary. Of course, there is always that medical locker room wisecrack: "The chance to cut is the chance to cure." But what if the cutting wasn't really necessary to begin with?

Just take a quick look at some comparative figures: England and Wales have just about half the number of surgeons we do—proportionately, that is. As a result, where these is one operation for every thirteen Americans there is one operation for every twenty-six people in England and Wales. Since there has never even been the faintest suggestion that the British don't get enough surgery—or that anyone there is denied needed surgery, we must be getting far too much. In fact, the individual qualified American surgeon averages only 3.8 operations (and this includes the minor ones as well as the major ones) each week—about half of what a British surgeon does. In short the individual American surgeon tends to be underprepared since he doesn't get the chance to do enough work to keep at peak performance. American surgeons want to do more surgery and perhaps even advise operations which they might not if they were kept adequately busy.

It's unfortunate but true that much surgery (such as tonsillectomies, appendectomies, gall bladder and hernia operations) depends for its frequency essentially on the numbers of surgeons and hospitals available. Dr. Charles E. Lewis, a University of California (Los Angeles) professor of preventive medicine, has proven that these operations are performed three or four times as often in some regions of Kansas as in others—and the frequency is directly dependent on the number of hospital beds and surgeons available.

But the problem lies with our whole society as well as the medical profession. We have a disproportionate number of surgeons here, but Great Britain trains only as many specialists as are actually needed. There are more neurosurgeons in Massachusets alone than in all of England and Wales with a population eleven times that of Massachusetts. Since neurosurgeons do a lot of the back surgery, this oversupply may account for some of the unnecessary surgical attacks made on the defenseless spines of America.

Back pain is about as frequent as the common cold—and certainly it takes more of a toll in time lost from work, in insurance costs (we all foot the bill for the insurance and compensation costs either through increased taxes and insurance premiums or just rising prices), in major health problems such as back surgery or hospitalization or a life of disability. It's been estimated that half a million Americans suffer disabling back injuries while at work and no one really knows how many others do so at home. Our National Center for Health Statistics estimates that 7 million people right now are being treated for backaches—with some 2 million new sufferers being added each year.

If you've ever had a backache you know how miserable it can be. So it's not surprising that back operations have become increasingly common since the introduction of the so-called "laminectomy" some ninety years ago when the first of the neurosurgeons, Sir William Macewen (a professor of surgery at Glasgow University), removed a piece of the backbone, part of the spinal column, to relieve pressure on the spinal cord. Surgery has come a long way since this operation was first performed in 1883 but, despite all the refinements, this procedure still fails alarmingly often and can result in even more pain and torment when it fails. Here is one of the true shortcomings of conventional medicine and you might well learn a bit about it to protect yourself.

Your spinal column is a series of twenty-six bones or vertebrae (built like diamond solitaire rings stacked one on the other) with a hole running through their centers and a solid column of bone where the diamonds would be. The whole thing is about two or two and a half feet long, depending on your height. Through the center or hole runs your spinal cord, about twice the thickness of a pencil and enclosed and protected by three layers of soft tissue or meningeal membranes.

When it comes to pain, it's the discs that are the most commonly blamed. Between the twenty-six vertebrae are these much-maligned spinal or intervertebral discs. They are cushioning pads of cartilege and connective tissue, ranging from one- to three-quarters of an inch thick. Like the cross section of the trunk of a tree, each disc is layered, with a ring made of tough fibrous material and a soft gelatinous center or nucleus. These discs are vitally important in the way your backbone works, for their movement, their give, makes possible your bending and twisting. They act as shock absorbers, for without them every step would literally feel like pounding your head on the pavement, with the full force of the impact being carried up through your back.

And, finally, there are spaces between the vertebrae through which the nerves from your spinal cord reach the furthermost parts of your body—your arms and legs, your fingers and toes—so that you can make your body do what you want it to, or feel when you put your hand on a hot pot, for instance. Direct pressure on these nerve roots can produce unbearable pain—as when you were a kid and some other youngster pressed your "funny bone." (Actually this squeezes a main nerve against the bone of the elbow joint.)

The famous "herniated disc" or "ruptured disc" operation has caused far more back problems than it has corrected. A herniated disc is one where the fibrous ring has been torn and the soft central nucleus squeezed out until it presses on a nerve root, producing incapacitating pain. The traditional surgical approach is to do a partial laminectomy—to cut away part of the vertebra so that the doctor can get at the nucleus of the disc and scrape it away until the nerve is no longer being pressured (stopping that other kid from pressing your "funny bone").

Some of the most serious weaknesses of conventional medicine are typified in the treatment of back pain, where any spinal changes are almost automatically interpreted as being the cause of the pain and with surgery all too often following promptly and promiscuously. I recently studied the notes kept during 250 operations supposedly done for ruptured discs. Only six reported an actually ruptured disc! Two hundred and two merely described a degenerated disc (no cause for surgery). I couldn't tell from the notes whether the other forty-two patients really had herniated discs. I feel the results warrant the statement that 90 percent of the patients didn't have a ruptured disc—although they were operated on for this condition! I found notes to the effect that when X-rays show some slight defect, the surgery is performed because the patient's pain persisted. But pain is not a definite test of anything and could be due to any one of a host of other problems. Why this surgery happens is conjectural: to be charitable, one can assume that—like the physician who turns to medications—the surgeon, trained and comfortable in the use of the scalpel, turns to it automatically when faced with a problem.

Although surgery has been my way of making a living since I began to practice, I still want to perform less of it rather than more. When a patient now comes in with acute low-back pain, I generally have him up and around after only a single day of bed rest—none of this two-week immobility, for it makes the patient stiff. His muscles hurt and there is danger of blood clots and phlebitis, even blood clots on the lung.

My active program of pain control (and all pain control is faith healing—for without the patient's faith in the doctor there can be no success) with electrical stimulation, ice, injections of local anesthetics, even acupuncture, is 90 percent successful. I've had to operate on only three or four discs in two years—and I see all the bad pain problems.

When the first operation fails, more operations are likely.

The scalpel is used to cut, starting with the local nerves at the site of the pain (say the nerve supplying a hand or a cheek or scalp). Sometimes this gives immediate relief but, surely and inevitably, it fails to last and the surgeon moves back to where the main nerve enters through the spinal disc to reach the spinal cord itself. Here he cuts the nerve root as it's about to enter the spinal column, catching more nerves and causing more unpleasant side-effects (strange numbnesses and perhaps loss of the use of a muscle or even a part such as a limb or the bladder).

But this too fails and then comes the cordotomy—cutting that section of the spinal cord through which the pain nerves are thought to travel to the brain itself. Yes, I said "thought" for if this were really so, cutting would end all pain permanently because these nerves can't regenerate. Sometimes today my colleagues even go in and burn with electrocauteries to avoid cutting too much. Here, too, there are serious side-effects with strangely painful reactions and even loss of such vital functions as bladder and bowel control—and the loss of sexual potency for the man. But, most tragic of all, if the patient survives for a year or more, the pain is likely to come back—and we have no idea why.

When cordotomy, too, has failed, the worst surgery of all is attempted by the doctor who is utterly committed to the knife—for now some surgeons will turn to lobotomies or other forms of psychosurgery. For example, pellets are buried in the brain and heated by radio waves so that they become intensely hot and actually burn away bits of the brain tissue. But this as we have already seen destroys the very soul of the human being, leaving him without many emotions, a flat empty shell of a human being—and the pain may still come back! But often the victims of psychosurgery are so damaged mentally that they don't mind the pain even though they feel it.

So we are left with two medical approaches—conventional, traditional medicine (the kind that most people are accustomed to and certainly the one most familiar to most physicians) and the exciting new occult medicine (the unconventional or alternative brand that seems so strangely unique even though it has existed far longer than today's conventional kind).

Which way should you go? To which kind do you turn when a problem arises? What should be your guideposts? These are the questions I want to look at with you next.

IV

The Practical Aspects of Occult Medicine

11

When to Use Conventional Medicine... and When the Occult

We've seen the weaknesses of conventional medicine and, heaven knows, they are many. But—like it or not—your very life depends on this ancient and traditional profession. Condemn it if you will for its many faults and weaknesses, the loss of its old-time ideals, the failure all too often of some of its members to adhere to the old Hippocratic ideal of doing good and not harm. But with all its weaknesses and problems—of both the profession as a whole and many of its individual members—this ancient profession is still your chief bulwark against illness and death. Surgery, despite all its excesses, still saves lives daily as it always has. Prescriptions, though handed out far too promiscuously, do save lives, as well as turn the unbearably tormented life into a livable one.

But as the Bible and the folk song say, to all things under the sun there is a season. And this is just as true of the use of conventional as of occult medicine. The question that bothers most patients is, "When should I cry 'Doctor'?" The answer is, "When you're sick."

For the physician must *always* be the first resort—and the need is astronomical. During 1972 alone, almost half a billion acute illnesses or injuries (448,600,000 to be exact) struck the civilian and non-institutionalized population of the United States: every American man, woman, and child got sick enough to require either medical help or a day or more of limited activity at least twice that same year; and some 32 million patients were discharged from hospitals after spending a total of 245 million days there. The American Medical Association found that during 1970 each general practitioner was coping with, on the average, some 175 patient-visits a week in which this same GP put in between 52 and 85 hours of work.

An acute illness is one which strikes swiftly and is of short duration. A chronic disease is one that lingers on for long periods or indefinitely (such as arthritis or migraine or diabetes). It's the acute physical illnesses that are truly the province of conventional medical care, for modern American medicine is spectacularly successful with these. The acute physical problem is also most appealing to doctors for it affords them the opportunity to utilize all their training and show their expertise, to conquer a difficult problem, to save a life, even to be heroic.

One recent study showed that almost 90 percent of the acute problems brought to doctors are relatively minor upper respiratory infections (colds, sore throats, sinus infections, etc.), along with conjunctivitis ("pink eye") and middle-ear infections.

In the really major acute problems such as strange and often deadly infections, bizarre symptoms, life-threatening injuries, breakdowns, or such conditions as heart attacks, strokes, or many kinds of tumors, doctors are at their best. They're trained to spot the problem, and they have a wide variety of powerful therapies, of drugs and facilities (coronary care units, kidney dialysis, etc.) with which to preserve and prolong life.

But, tragically, they find that the greatest bulk of their patients they *cannot* help. In one way it's fortunate that these are the patients whose disorders are usually neither life-threatening nor dangerous but this very fact increases the doctor's impatience with such problems when there are so many other sufferers with really serious conditions, the acute kinds that can and do kill—and that can be helped and are interesting. Perhaps this tends to make doctors treat the nonacute sufferers with some degree of contempt.

Yet these chronic patients surely do suffer with dis-ease, surely do need some form of medical help to restore them to healthy, normal, productive lives. Among these are the chronic complainers and the psychosomatic sufferers which medical students are warned about but never taught to handle. Here the prescription is tried (sometimes a sugar pill, most often a tranquilizer or sedative or even a narcotic for pain)—and virtually always fails. Nothing more helpful is provided in conventional medicine.

Let me repeat once more: *every* medical problem *must* be diagnosed by a physician. *Don't* try self-diagnosis! Only the doctor can diagnose your condition—he may not have the tools for treating it but he surely is the best protection you can find, the only one prepared to diagnose both the problem and its cause, and to call in the help of the occult when this is warranted or needed. But the big question to most people is when does one see a doctor. Of course you're not going to run to a physician with every minor cold or bellyache. But *you should seek medical help every time you have something that isn't normal or usual, and which lasts.* If you've never had a headache and suddenly get a blazing one, you should consider seeing a doctor—and certainly should if it's still present the next day as well.

If you've been suffering with tension or migraine headaches for the past thirty years you're not likely to worry—though you may be miserable—if you get one more. If I had a marked pain in my leg "out of the blue" and it was gone in an hour or two, I'd forget it—but if it lasted all day and I got up the next morning with it still there, I'd be concerned. I'd certainly seek help if it continued all that day too, or if it went away but kept coming back.

When I speak of "out of the blue" this is what I mean: if my leg hurt after putting in two hours of tennis for the first time in the season I wouldn't consider that "out of the blue" but I would if I'd sat around all day and suddenly my pain started. In short, if my usual health pattern is changed, I'd seek medical help promptly. If I were accustomed to getting cramps or diarrhea when I was upset, this wouldn't worry me unduly—but if it occurred at a time it never had before or if there were blood present, I would surely look for medical help.

The first source of help should be a good doctor when any physical problem is present. A really competent and well-trained family doctor can diagnose and handle almost all of your medical problems and can tell when you need the care of a specialist. The new family practitioner, today's scientific version of the old GP, is even being trained to handle most obstetrics cases as well as most of the problems now being referred to the specialist.

Most of all, these younger men and women—and most family practitioners now being trained are young—are being taught the importance of love, the "bedside manner" and I think this is a very hopeful sign for the future. It's my impression that these young people are very open to occult medicine and are likely to use the help of psychics or develop their own psychic abilities to provide the faith healing that the old GP did so automatically when he had neither effective drugs nor technology to hide behind.

There are two kinds of medical problems—those that are basically physical (although all physical problems do carry with them some emotional disturbance, if only anxiety over the condition itself) and those that are psychosomatic or the result of some psychological reaction to stress or of some condition which produces a physiological effect (as for example, thinking of food will make your mouth water). But in any case, there is only one place for your initial diagnosis—your own doctor—but where you can best find help depends on the kind of problem involved.

Let's look for a moment at some for-instances. There are some disorders we suffer that are pretty much physical. The emotional components are few and usually a reaction to the physical problem. If Bill fractures his leg he has a physical problem which will require a mechanical type of physician (an orthopedic surgeon) to repair the damage. However, even here there is an emotional component for Bill will be upset by his pain and his inability to function as usual. Bill may feel anxiety about the cause of the accident (a fall or slip perhaps, an auto accident) or be worried about surgery or general anesthesia. But his doctor will quickly provide relief from pain with an analgesic, and set Bill's leg.

Harold wakes up with a pain in his eye such as he had not dreamed possible. The eyeball is red and feels hard as a stone. His doctor quickly sends him to an ophthalmologist, who diagnoses the condition as acute glaucoma and promptly performs emergency surgery; Harold's sight is saved.

Larry was sent to a hospital coronary care unit when he developed chest pain, only to be discharged in a couple of days. A false alarm. But had Larry's pain been a real heart attack this prompt medical care by his physician would very likely have saved his life.

Sophie's doctor found a polyp during the examination of her colon, which is done routinely on many patients over the age of forty by family practitioners. The growth was removed quickly and simply—and a cancer perhaps prevented.

All of these examples clearly show why you should seek your physician when you have a symptom or disorder—or just for your regular examination. And if you have diabetes, your doctor's orders can preserve your life. I know of a spiritual healer who urged his client not to take her insulin as a proof of her belief in his healing. Her husband came home one day to find her dead on the floor as a result of her failure to follow her doctor's prescribed insulin therapy. She was a fool, and so was her healer. *Your doctor is there to protect you: follow his or her orders and treatment— regardless of what else you do or what other help you seek in addition.*

So let me summarize: *FIRST SEEK COMPETENT MEDICAL CARE* for any ailment. Then, *FOLLOW YOUR MEDICAL ADVICE*—it's worth your life. Other help (such as prayer, faith healing, the occult) is very valuable—but only when there is no risk. Don't, for example, let someone with a heart attack sit around while you're seeking faith healing for him. Get *immediate* medical attention. While the victim is in a good coronary care unit with the best possible medical care, then you can seek the additional help from the occult that may well tip the balance in his favor. It can, and often does, turn the whole picture around. But *always* get the best medical care you can. This goes for cancer, arthritis, diabetes, appendicitis, or for any physical disease or disorder you suffer.

But let us go on to examine "functional" disorders—changes in the way the body works, not diseases which attack the body in a physical way, though they may cause physical symptoms. There is a change in the way the body functions. Thus in hay fever the nose runs but there is no real change in the tissues of the nose; it is only overproducing a normal material. Your stomach lining normally produces acid to digest your food but an overproduction of acid can burn a hole in that very lining and so produce a stomach ulcer. If this burning continues until it hits a blood vessel you get the so-called "bleeding ulcer." An ulcer is a physical problem even though the original "cause" was psychological tension.

It is with psychosomatic diseases that conventional medicine is most often helpless. They are most likely to be chronic, for they are part of the whole lifestyle the individual develops for various reasons (such as the circumstances of early life or just copying the parents' patterns) and then tends to follow—not necessarily consciously—throughout life. He may, for example, react to anger or anxiety or pressure by developing what was once termed, medically, mucous colitis—gripping intestinal cramps from increased intestinal activity.

When my associate, Arthur Freese, was in dental practice he specialized in headaches and saw a great many patients referred by physicians for this problem. He recalls Jerry, a teenager who got a headache every time he faced an examination. Jerry just got so tense that the muscles in the back of his neck went into spasm—which he suffered as severe headaches.

Of course, psychosomatic problems need not be chronic; the middle-aged businessman I once saw certainly had an acute one. He was doubled up with abdominal pain which came on in waves during the last three days of a tense and particularly important— but unsuccessful—business trip. It was the first time he'd suffered this particular psychosomatic manifestation of anxiety. Our modern term for it, "irritable colon syndrome" (a syndrome is a collection of symptoms), is much more accurate than the old "mucous colitis" because there may be any of a number of symptoms (cramps, diarrhea, constipation, mucous in the stool).

The conventional medical treatment of this syndrome is sedatives, tranquilizers, and even analgesics—and, again, the patient can be in danger of habituation and even possible addiction. Here, then, is the ideal place for the use of the occult—a condition which is benign and where there are no physical changes in the body (though the disorder is *felt* physically by the patient), where the problem is really only an exaggerated amount of perfectly normal healthy activity, where there is pain without damage; a condition which medication only temporarily relieves, and at a serious risk—without treating the underlying problem.

There are other chronic problems that are really the bane of the physician's existence. He or she feels inadequate and uncomfortable, unable to cope successfully through conventional medical methods.

One such problem is the form of arthritis which results from wear and tear—osteoarthritis, the most common form. Virtually everyone past the age of forty has it to some degree.

Another such problem is the headache. We don't even understand the cause of migraines.

The problem of chronic pain is virtually in a class by itself. The chronic pain patient typically plays his own pain game and creates a world in which his pain is the central factor, dominating and distorting all his life and relationships, destroying his own life and that of his family and even manipulating his doctors. Yet only very rarely is there enough physical disease or pathology to account for the amount of pain reported. To almost all these patients normal activity can only do good, not harm. Yet the pain prevents a normal life.

Finally there are those conditions which are lost causes, for which no conventional medical help is available, where the patient has to be written off as medically hopeless—terminal cancer, strange disorders such as multiple sclerosis, and some cases of arthritis where functioning is terribly limited and medicine can do nothing to help the underlying condition.

As I see it, the role of conventional medicine is all-pervasive, even though, unfortunately, it is severely limited in its overall efficacy at this time. Medicine must be used for its diagnostic abilities and its great healing power in many areas. The physician *must* be consulted first and his continuing care is essential so that every conventional medical help is kept available and continued: such things as antibiotics and insulin; hormones and drugs to reduce terribly high blood pressure; hospital facilities for heart attacks; the fantastic new open-heart surgery; the drugs which protect for long periods or even permanently after heart attacks; and the new cancer therapies (everything from chemicals and the "atomic cocktails" for thyroid tumors to the radiation often so effective and surgery, still the most effective weapon against this dread disease).

It is important of course—I stress again!—to continue under the care of the doctor until you are dismissed. But there is a whole other world slowly opening up for you, which takes up where traditional medicine leaves off—and which, I predict, will become part of the medical profession. Physicians will use occultists as they now use paramedical personnel to carry out radiotherapy. But today the occult is not generally available so you have to put up with the next best—keeping in contact with your doctor while seeking help from occult medicine.

The occult must provide help in which there is *no* risk—and medical care must not be discontinued until the doctor finds you healed and no longer in need of conventional help.

In La Crosse, a prayer or two with some hand movements over a photograph and I am told the hole in the child's head will heal within six months. In Baltimore, a man is told, "You don't have appendicitis, your gallbladder is filled with stones." And in New York—over the phone—a witch assures my associate, in spite of his belief, that his injured ankle isn't broken. All three of these clairvoyant predictions (one was faith healing, the other two were psychic diagnoses) proved to be accurate! Clearly this is a real force to be reckoned with, a powerful ability or talent or gift or whatever it is. I have been fortunate enough to see occult medicine in action in many places in our country—and in other countries as well.

I think occult medicine is the most dramatic, exciting, and provocative aspect of medical care today, the one with the greatest potentiality—if only because it's the least developed and explored. It includes such seemingly strange approaches as teaching people to control their own inner bodily workings just as the yogis of the East do—to slow the heart rate or lower the blood pressure, even to control epileptic seizures. This is the approach of biofeedback and autogenic training, twin manifestations of the same process.

It does seem odd that traditional medicine today should look down on the occult—for only yesterday the occult *was* medicine, and anything available then was what we would regard as unconventional today. Astrology and mystic divinations, spells and incantations, magic formulas (remember how warts were said to cured by throwing a cat over the fence or saying certain verses in the dark of the moon?) were respected medical practices.

But with the advent of superscientific rationality, a strange pattern began to form. Instead of being combined and unified, the varied medical practices were separated. What was considered rational and scientific became "right." The mystic, the occult, found itself regarded as "wrong," something to be sneered at, ashamed of, vigorously condemned. But in the victory of rationalism much was lost—for had we paid attention to the lessons and practices of the past, to folk wisdom and folk medicine, we would have had many of our most powerful scientific drugs long before we did.

Antibiotics, for example, were used long before Sir Alexander Fleming stumbled on penicillin. One middle-aged Ohio woman recalls that her grandmother, half a century ago, applied mildewed bread to superficial infections. The use of moldy materials—food or soil or other vegetable matter—and of extracts of lichens goes back to the very earliest folk medicine. Moldy bread was used for skin infections by the ancient Egyptians. Yet the world had to wait until 1939 when Rene Dubos sparked the interest in antibiotics.

And then of course there is rauwolfia—reserpine, we call it. First introduced into Western medicine in 1952, it's a powerful sedative and tranquilizer, effective against high blood pressure (hypertension) and psychoses (insanity). This drug, so new to us, is actually a very old and familiar one in Hindu medicine; extracts of rauwolfia were used by the ancient Hindus some 4,000 years ago—for hypertension, emotional problems, and psychoses!

Don't forget the toad's skin which, since the dawn of recorded history, has been used in magical potions and mystic rituals by witch doctors and sorcerers. Before you either shudder at the thought of eating it or laugh at the superstition involved, stop and recognize along with today's pharmacologists and other drug specialists, that toads are diverse biochemical and drug factories. Toad skin, for example, produces a whole range of powerful drugs which have an action on the heart similar to that of digitalis. The ancients didn't often miss a trick, for toads also produce a hallucinogenic substance. Perhaps those canny old witch doctors deliberately used this for kicks or to send their long-suffering patients on a wild trip.

And then there are the plants, leaves, or berries which are natural sources of the salicylates (the drug family from which comes our own highly effective aspirin). These have been used since the Stone Age. Hippocrates used willow leaves (a good source of salicylates) to relieve the pain of childbirth. The Roman soldiers of those days used various parts of the willow tree to relieve both their pain and their fever.

The poppy with its opium has also been used by suffering man since the Stone Age, and has never gone out of style.

I often wonder—and sadly—how much we have lost and are currently missing by discarding current and ancient myths and beliefs, ignoring the folk tales, and rejecting the rich folk medicine so laboriously built up over tens of thousands of years. We laugh at the strange diets and medications used by practitioners of the occult. How many "miracle drugs" are buried in the herbs or strange concoctions they recommend?

We have even forgotten the things that our own grandparents did for pain or sickness, ignoring such things as poultices and the influence of the moon.

Modern scientists have just recently begun to recognize the vastness of lunar influence. While everyone knows that ocean tides are produced by the gravitational forces of the moon, only a tiny handful of specialists like Drs. Anthony Lambert and Don Bower, Canadian government scientists (spring 1974 issue of *Geos*): ". . . realize that the ground beneath their feet moves up and down approximately twice a day through a distance of one or two feet." In fact our earth is not a globe, but an oblate spheriod, because of being pulled by the moon. If the moon can do that to solid ground, we need not be surprised to find it has great influence on our bodies and our behavior—as the astrologers have always known. Using astrology, we can know the best times to take drugs and the proper time for surgery—when conditions are favorable for both the patient and the operating team.

The old, the folk medicine of the past, clearly has much to offer. With our modern scientific techniques we can prove or disprove the ancient beliefs. Out of a rich heritage of drugs and concepts we can save those which have a real basis and convert them into useful and precise medical tools with which to help suffering humanity.

Today's American physician just hasn't been adequately trained to help what are all too often referred to in hospital locker room discussions as the "crocks"—those who complain of nonphysical ailments which do not readily yield to the methods with which our doctors feel most comfortable. "Crocks" or no, people who suffer need help, and the occult and its practitioners can help them.

Moreover, much of the occult is safe to use in those cases where the psychosomatic disorder does not represent a threat to life. Hayfever, for example, is not life-threatening. On the other hand, ulcers must be regularly checked by a doctor because they may bleed.

Certainly help from occult medicine is in order when the doctor says, "There is no hope—we've done all we can do." Even worse, he may say, "It's only a matter of time," (in cases of terminal cancer, tumors that don't respond to treatment, late-stage heart or kidney disease, etc.).

There are other diseases, such as multiple sclerosis, in which hope is only slight at best and medical therapies are virtually impotent. There are painful conditions like arthritis or disfiguring ones like psoriasis in which medicine is still relatively ineffective.

To sum up: get adequate and immediate medical or surgical care to preserve life. Conventional medical or surgical care is the first essential for this. The doctor's diagnosis and ongoing care are vital.

But I have seen patients who know they are dying, and know that conventional physicians cannot heal them. Shouldn't we in the medical profession take the lead in freeing these people to seek one last hope? If the medical profession itself would lead the way, then we could really claim the title "healer." We should keep up any needed medical care while urging them to seek that one final hope—whether it be a trip to Lourdes or a serious faith healer who has a record of successes. Even if the occult works with only one in ten, one in a hundred, one in a thousand—perhaps this sufferer will be the one! (Actually the really good faith healers have a surprisingly high success rate.)

And doctors should *not* try to mask functional disorders with tranquilizers and sedatives, or bury pain with narcotics. Drugs are the wrong answer, because the patients end up with an addiction that's even worse than their "functional" problem. Why not try a faith healer here too? With medical supervision nothing can go wrong, and the patient may even recover. I think it's disgraceful for physicians—supposedly healers—to sneer at faith healers and say, "They only cure the psychosomatic disorders." Even if that were true, faith healers would be effective with the great bulk of medical problems. What's more, the patient with "psychosomatic" pain hurts just as much as the one with a fractured skull or arthritis.

As for me, I'm a physician to heal, to help, to relieve suffering—not to pass superficial moral judgments on which patients I should concern myself with and which ones I should ignore. I still want to try anything that might tip that fragile sensitive balance between life and death toward life.

We are going to be talking about some of these other wonders in the next chapters.

New Occult
Medical Practices:
Acupuncture, Biofeedback,
and Autogenics

You live in a new world of space travel, nuclear energy, détente, coexistence with Communism, hair styles of past centuries, and lifestyles of those yet to come. Like you, doctors feel strain, divided loyalties, throwbacks to the past, and glimpses into the future. Today's ambivalent and confused doctors find themselves having to evaluate the use of simple needles, ultrasophisticated electronic gadgets—and the power of the mind itself.

We may now be moving to a stage in which we will gain better control of the innermost automatic functioning of our bodies, such as our heartbeat, our blood circulation, and our intestinal workings. Yogis have this control to varying degrees but there are now only a few of them. In the future we may all acquire such control. Dr. Paul Dudley White himself, while only a young doctor, dipped into the very biofeedback and autogenic training or transcendental meditation which we today regard as something very new. Through this form of occult medicine, I believe many sufferers can be helped—those with Raynaud's disease (which can lead to gangrene of whole areas of the extremities), headaches, muscle tension, high blood pressure, too-rapid heartbeat, and even epilepsy.

What other mysteries, miracles, and magic do new health practices offer today? Let's look at these as well as at their drawbacks. Some can kill. Some are questionable. Some belong only in expert hands. Some are simple, safe, and easy.

Acupuncture has been around for a long long time. Chinese tradition has it that their Yellow Emperor or August Lord, Huang-ti, devised acupuncture some 5,000 years ago. But even Huang-ti (later to become the patron saint of Taoism) was a latecomer, for stone acupuncture needles from the Stone Age have been found in China.

Chinese acupuncture is a truly occult and mystic combination of philosophical and religious beliefs combined with simple observations. Good and ill health are thought to depend on the relative strengths of two forces: the *Yin* (the northern side of a mountain—negative, cold, dark, and female) and the *Yang* (the southern side—positive, light, warm, and male). The body's organs are classified as "storage" or "passive" ones (*Yin*) and the "working" or "active" ones (*Yang*).

The *Yin* and *Yang* must be kept in balance for health. When this equilibrium is disturbed there is sickness. Acupuncture allows excess Yin or Yang to escape and so restores balance—and, with it, health. Gold, silver, copper, brass, steel, or iron needles are used. The number of the so-called acupuncture points (where the needles are inserted) has increased with the centuries. Some sources describe 295 points, others 365. Many others record totals running into the 600s or even the 700s, and some talk of more than 1,000.

The acupuncture points which affect a particular organ are believed to be connected by invisible channels—meridians—containing the *Yang* and the *Yin*. There were first thought to be twelve meridians. Then eight "special meridians" each with its own acupuncture points were added. With time, another twelve "extra meridians" were added, plus another group affecting the skin and muscles which were classified as "muscular meridians." Some of the points are believed to correspond to the five elements—metal, wood, earth, fire, and water.

In acupuncture theory, the body corresponds in various ways to the universe and even to the state. But here you get involved in considerations so esoteric and metaphysical that I, for one, am hopelessly lost. If you're interested, you'll have to find your own way through all this without me—I stick to the aspects of acupuncture useful to me.

In any case, acupuncture has been widely practiced in China since the Stone Age. It was introduced into Europe by a Dutch surgeon toward the end of the seventeenth century and has had many adherents there ever since. It never took hold here in America until *New York Times* columnist James Reston reported on his experience with acupuncture for relieving his post-surgical discomfort in China just a few years ago. Now, however, the practice has become so widespread that I find about a fourth of the patients who come to my pain clinic have already tried this ancient Chinese treatment before they seek my help. Clearly, large numbers of people with a variety of medical problems are turning to this new-to-Americans therapy. I am glad of their open-mindedness but there are things about it that you should know for your own protection. You must know the good *and* the bad.

Acupuncture can and does kill or seriously injure—as does almost any medical or surgical procedure. A series of recent case reports in the June 17, 1974, issue of the *Journal of the American Medical Association (JAMA)* highlights this fact. As with any other procedure, safety or danger to a very considerable extent depends on the care, training, and expertise of the operator as well as on the precautions instituted to protect the patient should something inadvertently go wrong. Let's look at a few instances to understand the problem.

One woman tried a little self-acupuncture. She inserted the needles into her chest, penetrated one of her heart's vital arteries, and killed herself. While this may seem unusual, a freakish rarity, it isn't as rare as it should be. A leading professor of anesthesiology, Dr. John J. Bonica of the University of Washington in Seattle, also tells of deaths from needles striking the heart. He also cites other major complications from acupuncture treatments, including collapsed lungs, damage from needle breakage, heart disorders, penetration of the pregnant uterus and the urinary bladder, and injuries to liver, spleen, and kidneys.

In the same issue of *JAMA*, a team of physicians from the University of Virginia Medical Center and George Washington University Medical Center in Washington, D.C., reported on their own cases. Patients who had been treated by acupuncturists included a fifty-eight-year-old woman who had had needles placed in her back. Difficulty in breathing and chest pain brought her to the hospital where almost a pint of blood had to be drained from her chest. She spent two weeks there with a partially collapsed lung, pneumonia, and a wound infection. A forty-five-year-old man with long-standing asthma gave up the steroids his doctor had prescribed and tried acupuncture. During his sixth treatment he suddenly began to struggle for breath. His life was saved by a physician who quickly administered oxygen and adrenalin for an acute allergic shock reaction and sent him by ambulance to a nearby hospital intensive care unit.

One of the problems here is simply that in Washington, D.C., (and a very few states) acupuncturists need *not* be physicians. Without a knowledge of anatomy (among other things) the acupuncturist can and does injure. *Acupuncture should be administered only by doctors who have been properly trained in it.*

There has been a rush toward this therapy which can be harmful unless performed under careful and limited circumstances. *Newsweek* reported only recently that a correspondence course in acupuncture was being offered by a Chinese and an Australian operating out of a Canadian shopping center. The course cost $1,650 and included a trip to Hong Kong for actual practice. The magazine reported that 200 pupils, including some thirty-odd U.S. doctors, had been attracted.

Clearly the asthmatic victim of acupuncture I cited above would have lost his life had there not been a physician available to diagnose his problem and institute prompt life-saving measures, and had there not been access to a hospital with its backup facilities and highly trained personnel.

There are basically two different uses of acupuncture. One shows promise and certainly demands much more scientific investigation to put it on a systematized and better-utilized basis. The other—with its offer of help for almost everything that ails you—has virtually no scientific evidence to support it and only a vague and highly suspect ancient theory behind it.

The most thorough American study of acupuncture is that of Dr. J. J. Bonica, chairman of the Ad Hoc Committee on Acupuncture of the National Institutes of Health and the American Society of Anesthesiologists. Dr. Bonica spent three weeks in China at the invitation of the Chinese Medical Association. He visited six cities, five medical schools, fourteen hospitals, three research facilities, and several communes, health resorts, villages, and industrial plants. He also reviewed the medical literature on acupuncture.

Dr. Bonica has followed this up with an even more recent report (*JAMA*, September 2, 1974) devoted to the use of acupuncture for anesthesia in surgery. His findings introduce, in my opinion, a healthy element of reality into this overheated argument. While he recognizes that operations in China are being performed with acupuncture as the anesthetic, he also finds that this procedure is *not* as frequent or as effective as the Chinese and earlier American visitors claim. Similar conclusions have been reached by our own Dr. Michael De Bakey and anesthesiologists from Switzerland, Austria, and Australia. Dr. De Bakey feels that we need much more scientific study to find what place this technique of anesthesiology is likely to have in surgery. I personally would feel that this is the time for *experimental use only* in surgery until we have the final facts.

Dr. Bonica's reports are scholarly and scientific. He finds that there's an appalling *lack* of scientific data accumulated by doctors in China to document their claims about how much or how well acupuncture works. In many Chinese health stations and even some hospitals there are *no* records kept of either the patient's history or the effect of treatment. Much Chinese acupuncture was done by "barefoot doctors," little-trained native practitioners, but they and the Western-style doctors do agree on one thing—that acupuncture will *not* really help the pain of cancer.

Dr. Bonica could find *no* real proof that acupuncture relieves deafness (and recent American reports confirm with objective audiograms or hearing tests that this therapy produces *no* improvement in the hard of hearing). He found patients suffering from high blood pressure, asthma, diabetes, and psychiatric illnesses treated with acupuncture—*along with* medications and familiar modern therapeutic procedures. Thus, high blood pressure was attacked with the usual needles along with herbs and reserpine (a drug we use in America); mental illnesses were treated with acupuncture, herbs, tranquilizers, and group therapy. In short, the Chinese are using the very holistic healing concept—*everything that might possibly work*—that I have already mentioned.

I can only join Dr. Bonica in his conclusions. He believes that acupuncture may well find a place in American medicine— for it does relieve pain. He sees no absolute scientific proof that acupuncture is more effective than placebos (which, as we have already seen, are remarkably effective), nor can he find any final proof that it is as effective as claimed for the many diseases for which it's being used.

I studied acupuncture with London's Dr. Felix Mann, generally regarded as the most accomplished Western acupuncturist. Acupuncture training should be thorough. A quickie lecture course with a couple of demonstrations doesn't equip anyone to perform this therapy, which is why I urge its teaching only in formal academic situations. Any physician can learn this, but he should only practice it after proper medical training. I feel it should be included in today's medical school training.

I have found acupuncture effective against pain in about 30 percent of my patients, much more so in acute pain than in chronic. But I would not use it for anything other than pain, until more definitive proof becomes available. However, like Dr. Bonica, I heartily agree with the many Western-style Chinese physicians he met who recognized the need for careful scientific studies and clinical tests—but who also pointed out how much of our Western medicine too is empirical—simple trial and error. If something seems to work we use it, even without scientific proof.

Whether it's doctors I'm lecturing to, or a patient in my office, the question I get is always the same: "What does acupuncture really feel like?" Well—first off, it hurts! Don't let anyone tell you it doesn't, for it just won't work unless it does. The needles themselves are very fine, about one one-hundredth of an inch in diameter, but they can be up to four inches long. I put them a half inch to inch into the patient, then twirl or twist them a full turn in each direction. Electroacupuncture is merely to take the strain off one's hands—the battery or current turns or vibrates the needles. The soreness that follows is so considerable that I give only two treatments a week at most because otherwise the patient becomes too sore. If you're in pain and don't get total relief lasting several days after your third treatment, you're just wasting your time thereafter and should look to other methods for relief.

The acupuncture now being practiced in the United States includes both the valuable and the worthless. More skepticism and science are needed. The sudden boom in this therapy is startling. Reporters for the well-known medical magazine *Medical World News* found that some acupuncture clinics claim to have treated as many as 6,000 and even 15,000 patients. Some handle more than 100 patients a day and others have as many as sixty people on their staffs. The acupuncture treatments are given for everything, these reporters found—from schizophrenia to shingles, from Parkinsonism to alcoholism, from sexual impotence to just about whatever you can name. Fees can run to $100 a treatment.

I feel I can best explain how I feel by telling what I would do if I were the patient. I personally would not have acupuncture for myself—except for pain. In pain, I think acupuncture can give striking relief in some cases. Above all else, I consider acupuncture—even for pain—*still experimental*. Much more research is needed before your doctor understands acupuncture as thoroughly as, say, penicillin or insulin. Yet only a physician can safely use acupuncture and even the physician should have had an extended course. I hope the medical schools will soon accept the responsibility for teaching acupuncture. Unlike faith healing (when used in conjunction with ordinary medical care) acupuncture *can* be harmful in untrained hands—and my test for the use of the occult is, can it harm?

Acupuncture isn't the only ancient discovery of the once-mysterious East which American medicine is now rediscovering. For when Dr. Paul Dudley White was only a resident at Massachusetts General Hospital (MGH) back in 1917, a young medical student told him that he could deliberately speed up his heartbeat. Always the open-minded medical scientist, the young doctor promptly marched the student off to his laboratory, hooked him up to an early version of the electrocardiograph, and told him to begin.

Dr. White recalled: "One second later his heart began to accelerate, and he reached a rate of 140 to 150 [normally it's about 70] within a few seconds by willpower. His pupils dilated. His blood pressure went up." Young Dr. White wrote a medical report on how this had all been done without any physical activity, just by some form of willpower. He heard that another student had performed a similar feat at the turn of century but he could find no one who remembered his name or what had happened to him so he stuck a note up on the MGH bulletin board requesting any available information on this old story.

A week later the Chief of Surgery at MGH came along. "I was the student," he said. Although he hadn't tried to speed up his heart in seventeen years he still managed to do so for Dr. White. Shortly before his death, Dr. White expressed open chagrin and disappointment that he had failed to see ahead more than half a century: "It seems so queer I didn't realize the importance of this fifty years ago."

Yet how could Dr. White have hoped to foresee that in the late 1960s Dr. Neal E. Miller, Rockefeller University professor, and his associates would teach rats to lower their heart rates from some 350 beats a minute to a mere 230; to make one ear blush and the other pale; to increase and decrease blood pressure, intestinal contractions, urine excretion, and the like. In short, all those bodily functions once thought to be beyond conscious control have been shown to be within our mental grasp—something the yogis, swamis, gurus, and other Eastern mystics have long known. Westerners have refused to believe it though British doctors of the last century brought back from India tales of yogis who stopped their hearts from beating, at will, and were even buried underground and dug up alive after a couple of weeks.

The achievements of yoga point us toward biofeedback and autogenics, the mechanical and the verbal aspects of the same phenomenon. Where biofeedback uses modern electronics, autogenics uses the simple basics of language and thought to achieve the same end, the control of body processes. Along with transcendental meditation, Zen, yoga, and other meditative disciplines, they work by some mechanism which is still not understood.

Let's look closely at biofeedback since it's the best known and so far the most scientifically and medically useful of these techniques. If you read the papers, the magazines, the books—or watch TV—you might begin to think everybody's "into alpha" these days, trying to find some personal Nirvana with the mind and a little black box. The field is loaded with cultists and phony gadgets which can no more tell you whether you're actually producing alpha waves than they can predict the next movement of the stock market or tomorrow's weather. Some faddists are trying to be mental athletes and others simply visceral ones. But there *are* serious investigators and there is real medical promise in biofeedback for it can correct disorders as different as asthma, epilepsy, stomach ulcers, migraine headaches, muscle tension, pain, and high blood pressure.

The ten billion nerve cells in your brain produce an electrical current which can be recorded by machines. To produce your brain's electrical current takes about as much power as a flashlight. Nobody really knows just how or why this electricity is produced. The device which detects these brain waves is called the *electroencephalograph* (EEG).

Relatively new to the public, the EEG was devised nearly half a century ago by a Bavarian, Dr. Hans Berger, who had studied physics and mathematics before turning to medicine. He eventually became director of the psychiatric clinic at Jena, Germany. In 1929 he first reported his results with a home-built EEG—and revolutionized medicine in general and the neurosciences in particular.

The device itself amplifies electrical current more than a million times so that it can detect, amplify, and record the tiny amounts of electrical current your brain generates. In the normal person this amounts to some one ten-thousandth of a volt and there are different levels of brain activity named by Berger from the Greek alphabet in the order in which he discovered them. He called the first one "alpha," the second "beta," and so on.

Alpha waves are those generated at 8 to 13 cycles per second, the beta at 14 to 25 per second, the theta 4 to 7 per second, and the delta 1 to 3 cycles per second. Sleep is delta, occasionally interrupted by bursts of faster waves. Delta may also arise from an area of localized brain tissue damage.

A safe, simple diagnostic tool such as the EEG gives those of us who are specially trained and interested in the functioning of the brain the exciting possibility of looking inside this organ in action, as it were. With EEG, we can diagnose and differentiate many brain problems—epilepsy, tumors, etc. Physical problems can be located and diagnosed, for later treatment with drugs or surgery—or occult medicine. The initial diagnosis and therapy *must* come from the physician—the neurologist or neurosurgeon—for misdiagnosis or even delay in diagnosis may well be fatal.

An epileptic seizure is virtually an electrical storm in the brain. Often the cause is unknown, but a common one may be injury. Setting off the seizure is a particular brain wave pattern.

Some biofeedback pioneers thought of the possibility of helping a patient set up different brain-wave patterns to block the epileptic pattern and prevent the seizure. Thus the EEG became not only a means of diagnosis but also a tool for control. Investigators in several laboratories have succeeded in teaching patients to control their own brain waves so that they can actually prevent or markedly reduce epileptic seizures. But this of course is not for amateurs. It should only be attempted by the most skilled and knowledgeable professionals and under close medical supervision. (However, emotional disturbances too can set off epileptic seizures and here psychics can help by reducing tension with their counseling—but, again, always under close medical supervision.)

When biofeedback is used to detect alpha waves, electrodes are attached to your head (by bands or glue) to transmit your brain's electricity to a black box where the current flashes a yellow or red or blue light, sounds a tone or beep, or makes a pen jiggle along a strip of paper. When the brain begins to produce alpha waves, the sound may stop or start or change in tone and the light may go on or off, flash, or change color. The signal tells you which brain wave you've achieved.

A similar system can be used to monitor your temperature, heart rate, blood pressure, the tension in your muscles, and almost every other bodily function. Biofeedback combines this monitoring with a device to feed the information back to you by means of sound or color or light or a graph. You learn—from the feedback—how to control your own reactions. Simple as all this sounds, it's such stuff as medical miracles are made of—truly occult medicine.

We know now that the mystics of the East really can control their bodies to an unbelievable degree, and we are learning to do the same though still only in a tentative, limited, halting fashion. Dr. Elmer E. Green, a Menninger Foundation Research Department director, recently reported his work with an Indian yogi. In Dr. Green's laboratory (shades of Dr. Paul Dudley White!) the yogi was able to jump his heart rate in one beat from about 70 a minute to some 300, stop his heart from pumping blood for 17 to 25 seconds, and produce three different brain wave types virtually at will. He could make two areas only a couple of inches apart on his palm warm and cool until there was about a 10° F. differential. This change took place at the rate of about 4° a minute: the left side of the palm became a rosy red and the right side an ashen gray. The yogi was practicing autogenic training since he didn't use a mechanical feedback device.

But this mystic isn't unique. Similar feats have been reported of many practitioners of yoga, Zen, and other forms of oriental meditation. One Indian yogi, for example, can produce sweat on his forehead within one and a half to ten minutes after being instructed to do so (his blood pressure shoots up simultaneously); others draw up water into their bladder or lower bowel through a catheter. During meditative states like these, alpha brain waves predominate.

The use of biofeedback with ordinary people has been exciting medically, with successes reported from all over the country.

In Denver, a team from the University of Colorado (Drs. Thomas Budzynski and Johann Stoyva) treated a twenty-nine-year-old woman who'd been suffering with day-long tension headaches for the past twenty years. Two or three times a week she would lie on a couch in the Denver psychologists' dimly lit laboratory with three electrodes pasted on her forehead and listen through earphones to a tone which rose or lowered with changes in her forehead muscle tension. After five months of this biofeedback, her headaches were virtually gone; she had learned to lower her muscle tension voluntarily. This work in Denver continues to produce successes.

In Topeka, Dr. Elmer Green and Dr. Joseph D. Sargent, a Menninger internist, put a temperature-measuring device on migraine sufferers' right index fingers and foreheads. When only the fingers were warmed, most migraines were relieved. One woman learned to raise the temperature of her hands 10° F. in two minutes. Dr. Charles F. Stroebel, director of psychophysiology at Connecticut's well-known Institute of Living, told Arthur Freese and me that he's able to bring relief to eight out of ten of his migraine patients using this Menninger technique.

In the summer of 1974, researchers at MGH used biofeedback to treat an old disorder called Raynaud's syndrome. Attacks of this disease begin at the fingertips and spread up the fingers and even the hands—and sometimes the toes and the nose are affected—with the parts turning white, cold, and pulseless. This may be followed by pain and a throbbing redness. It's caused by spasms of the arteries involved but the basic cause and treatment are both poorly understood. The disorder can last for years, after which gangrene may develop.

Starting with a thirty-one-year-old Boston man on whom all conventional methods of treatment had failed, an MGH team headed by Dr. Thomas P. Hackett, a Harvard psychiatry professor, tried biofeedback. With a temperature-monitoring device on his forefingers, the patient tried warming his hands while a training device emitted "beep" tones whose pitch rose with increasing hand temperatures. The first session was disappointing but by the fifth, temperatures in both hands could be raised more than 7°. This patient was the most successful of the seven in the experiment. The method failed in four cases.

The MGH group is planning to extend its biofeedback research to other problems. Dr. Hackett agrees with many of us who are trying this occult approach: "Biofeedback . . . may become one of the major treatments of the future for diseases that until now have been largely uncontrollable. And although this technique may change markedly . . . a whole new avenue of medicine has been opened."

Reports on biofeedback research also come from California, Florida, New England, Kansas, the Rocky Mountain states, New York City, Silver Springs, Maryland, and the U.S. Department of Defense. So extensive has the work become that I can only outline it here.

Patients are reported to be learning to speed up or slow down their heart rates and to eliminate heart irregularities. Blood pressure was lowered from 140 to 70 in one woman and varying amounts in others. The training has restored muscle function in people who've suffered paralysis of half the body or slight paralysis of the lower limbs. One young woman is said to have been able to reduce her epileptic seizures from two a month to a single one in the last six months. The Defense Department is said to be involved in teaching biofeedback to soldiers to keep their hands warm so they can work in cold climates without gloves and without frostbite, and even perhaps control the swelling and bleeding that occur after injuries. And at a recent meeting one research team reported that they could teach subjects to raise their scrotal temperatures to 104°—well above "normal." There was talk of the use of this strange ability as a new form of contraception, since sperm production is then curtailed for six weeks.

Essentially biofeedback, yoga, Zen, autogenic training and transcendental meditation seem to work in the same way although further research may reveal differences. However, we really don't know the internal body mechanisms which cause these changes suddenly to come under the conscious control of the mind. What we do know is that the people for whom this works (it won't work with everyone) seem to try various internal experiments until they finally stumble on the way to control their own bodies. They all describe the process differently. Some speak of it in terms of thoughts, others as emotions or feelings. Still others try to visualize a foot, say, and that it feels hot, the blood pouring through its blood vessels, and so on. And there are many who are quite successful in controlling their bodily functions but can offer no coherent verbal explanations or descriptions of how they do it.

In the May 1974 *Archives of General Psychiatry* came a voice on the other side, from the University of Mississippi Department of Psychiatry. It's always wise in medicine to listen to the opposite side, to question and hesitate. The Mississippi team, headed by Dr. Edward B. Blanchard, has critically reviewed biofeedback training and come to the conclusion (with which others, including me, will disagree no doubt) that only with tension headaches and the other problems which require muscle retraining (including paralysis) is there truly strong evidence for the efficacy of biofeed-back. In heart irregularities, blood pressure, epilepsy, Raynaud's disease, skin warming, and even the production of alpha brain waves, the team finds the evidence often very highly suggestive but also often inconclusive.

This team's conclusions seem valid to me. They bring a breath of strong scientific thinking into an area that is emotionally overheated at the moment, an area of much cultism and not enough experimental confirmation. Certainly the team is right that we are not yet able to proclaim biofeedback as the answer to all psychosomatic and other disorders; biofeedback is no panacea but is an intriguing and exciting tool which is certainly useful. It is close to proven for muscle retraining, and offers much hope and a fertile field for further investigation in many other areas of medicine.

Effective treatment of psychosomatic disorders, I feel, must involve the autonomic nervous system which does all our routine physiological housekeeping—keeps our hearts beating, lungs breathing, blood pressure up, kidneys working, and the like. If we had to pay conscious attention to these continuous functions, we wouldn't have any time left over for living; all our time would be spent making our bodies operate.

Autogenic training is a series of mental and verbal exercises in which the same mechanisms operate as in biofeedback, less suc-cessfully, perhaps because people tend to be more comfortable, at least in the United States, with machines than with just their own minds. Both of these techniques work through the hypothalamus which operates as a sort of switchboard in the brain for the au-tonomic system. By thinking, we can control this system and even-tually bring psychosomatic disorders under our control.

I like to tell my patients to concentrate on feeling the heart-beat in each part of the body, starting with the face. When you can feel your heart actually beating (say in your face or hand), you automatically get a dilation of the blood vessels in the particular part and it feels warm, and the autonomic nervous system has to slow down. You can tune and relax each part of your body sequentially, starting with your face and moving on to the neck, then the arms, the chest, and so on, down to your feet.

Another way of accomplishing this relaxation is to develop the feeling that your whole body has expanded by one inch. When this sensation has fully taken hold, it will necessarily cause you to relax. Then you expand your body by three inches, then by six, and so on until you reach a full twelve inches all over your body. You can't do this when you're tense, and so when you reach this feeling of expansion, you've relaxed fully.

I've found that a majority of chronic pain patients can control their pain by regular autogenic and/or biofeedback training.

I feel that combining biofeedback or autogenic training with the work of a psychic can help over 90 percent of the patients with psychogenic or psychophysiologic symptoms.

There is no better example than the boy in his late teens who came to me paralyzed from the waist down. He couldn't sit up for even fifteen minutes without agonizing pain. Going to college was impossible because he couldn't sit long enough to attend classes. I started by teaching him to put himself into an alpha state with a biofeedback machine. (Very few of these—and virtually none of the types available to the public—are worth anything). After seven weeks of regular practicing this young man could sit up 25 percent of the time—in comfort. In six months he had 75 percent control over his pain—and he was finally prepared to live an active life despite his paraplegia.

Relief for Your Pain:
Occult vs. Conventional

Everything about pain is unclear—even the very word "pain." It's confusing to patient and doctor alike. The stoutest heart may well quail before its terror. It haunts all our lives, starting with the pangs of birth and the hurt of being thrust alone and naked into a hostile, unknown world. It continues through the suffering from injury and illness, both physical and mental, off and on all the days of our lives until all too soon and perhaps in pain we depart. Nothing is truly certain about pain—except that we all dread it. A famous French surgeon, René Leriche, once said that the only pain that is truly easy to bear is the pain of others.

Almost all of medical practice is concerned with the diagnosis and treatment of pain. Pain is what brings patients to the doctor—the painful joint (arthritis), the painful head (migraine), the painful belly (appendicitis or a gallstone), the painful chest (pleurisy or a heart attack), the painful back or leg. It's pain that drives patients to their physi-cians—and until they get help it keeps them coming back.

Pain is tricky. What doctor can say how bad it is or even if it's really there or not? For we have no pain gauge to measure 6° or 4 ounces or 10 feet of pain. And pain can be many things—hurt feelings or terminal cancer, a broken leg or the terrible neuralgia following shingles, a toothache or a pinched finger, or the over-whelming pain of depression. Pain is only a convenient label we apply to a whole range of hurtful unpleasant experiences. Ordinar-ily pain is a symptom, a warning that something is wrong, and that we should attend to it. But sometimes pain is not just a warning but a disease in itself, which debases, disables, dehumanizes, and puts an end to normal life. Its victims are chronic invalids who spend most or all their days in bed or on a sofa, unable to contrib-ute to their own or anyone else's lives, a burden to themselves and to everyone around them.

The physician classifies pain as acute and chronic. Acute pain is sudden and unlikely to last long. With or without help, it will be resolved—the broken bone will heal, the heart attack will subside (or be fatal), the grit in the eye will either come out by it-self or be removed. Chronic pain is long-lasting as in arthritis, migraine headaches, the irritable colon syndrome, or muscle spasms.

Acute and chronic pain require different treatment and han-dling, vary in their effects on both patient and doctor, respond dif-ferently to medication, and differ in what kind of future they offer the sufferer.

As far as I know, I'm the first physician ever to specialize in and devote all my practice to the medical problems of pain. I have even helped coin the term "dolorologist" for those who specialize in the management of pain.

Today's conventional American doctors are at their finest when you turn to them with what they call "real" pain from actual pathology or disease.

Immediate relief is needed and they have a whole chestful of effective analgesics at their command. Then comes the work of tracking down the cause and eliminating it—removing the offending appendix, treating the middle ear abscess, or setting the broken bone. Conventional medicine can be magnificent at this job.

But chronic pain is a whole different problem—and one for which traditional American practitioners are totally unprepared. It really isn't their fault for they simply have never been given any training in chronic pain, either in diagnosis or in treatment. The whole medical education and our very culture are so organized that doctors feel inadequate, angry, and frustrated when they meet a problem which won't be cured by their familiar tools, a patient who doesn't play the medical game right, who won't stop hurting after the routine procedures.

Physicians feel that when they hand the patient a prescription, the patient should return the next visit and say, "It worked— no more pain!" But the chronic pain patient doesn't do that. He comes back with as much pain as when he left (or more!) and before the unsuspecting conventional doctors know it they're trapped into the game (as in the transactional analysis the late Dr. Eric Berne wrote about in *Games People Play*).

So Dr. Smith tries stronger drugs and Mrs. Jones comes back announcing, perhaps even triumphantly, "It still hurts." Dr. Smith feels challenged. The community and the Jones family look expectantly at Dr. Smith or say openly, "You have to do something to help her." He now prescribes stronger and stronger drugs and as the days stretch into weeks and months, Mrs. Jones becomes an addict without anyone—least of all Dr. Smith or Mrs. Jones—realizing it.

Or somewhere along the way Dr. Smith in desperation recommends surgery. But one operation like one narcotic only leads to the next and the next and so on—all without relief.

There are millions of Americans who suffer pain day and night. I turned to the study of pain because I felt there *had* to be a way to help them. Now there is hope for these sufferers—but in occult, not conventional medicine.

The typical chronic pain patient has had four operations on his back, has suffered pain for four to ten years—and has run up a medical bill of something like $75,000 before finally seeking help from my specialized facilities. I know of one sufferer whose medical bills ran close to half a million dollars! Almost two-thirds of my pain patients suffer with chronic low-back pain, and "disc surgery" has failed for them.

Let's look at a few of my patients. Jack was a man in his mid-fifties who for seven years (since his back surgery) had been confined to bed with pain which no drugs could alleviate. Bruce had injured his spine in sports practice and was also totally confined to bed and unable to work for five years. Martha had had four disc operations and a spinal fusion and been told by her doctor to do nothing at all. All—treated in different ways I'll shortly try to explain—are now functioning and living normal active lives.

The typical chronic pain patient is also addicted to drugs— opiates and their derivatives or synthetic (man-made) substitutes, tranquilizers, and sedatives. In a group of twenty-four patients entering my clinic at any one time, only one will be taking nothing stronger than aspirin. When they come in they are clinging desperately to the drugs upon which they have become dependent. Their makeup kits and briefcases are filled with drugs. One man had patches of ulcerated skin caused by too-frequent injections of analgesics. Another had drugs hidden in his boot. A woman had hers in her brassiere.

Conventional physicians are helpless with patients like these. In the treatment of chronic pain the American medical profession is at its weakest.

Not only have the doctors not been trained to handle the chronic pain problem, they've actually been taught how *not* to deal with it. For "scientific medicine" has eliminated the old bedside manner—the faith healing—and replaced it with impersonal laboratory tests and X-rays. Specialized "know-how" has been substituted for the love and psychological understanding of the healers of earlier centuries. Medical training prevents doctors from utilizing or developing their own natural psychic resources. They are further hampered by being too busy, by the harried desire to see more patients each day. Thus they have lost the most powerful instrument in their whole armamentarium—the love that chronic pain patients need, even more than any other group of sufferers.

This loss of love is another reason why medical facilities today should use the services of psychics—whether clairvoyants or faith healers—for they can spend the time necessary to understand the patient, inform the doctor of the patient's psychological problems, and even offer counselling.

In my pain clinic, I use Henry Rucker extensively for this purpose. One patient's husband told me, "Doc, he's the greatest thing you've ever found! Whatever you do, don't lose him!" This was after Henry sat down with this man and his wife whose pain problem had destroyed their personal, social, and sexual lives for ten years. Divorce seemed the only answer for these unhappy distraught people until Henry used his clairvoyant abilities to see their problems and by competent psychological handling turn them toward a more stable future.

The real difficulty with chronic pain problems is that the condition has been allowed to fester and grow for too long. No person can suffer severe pain for any length of time without changing physically and emotionally so that after even a few months you are no longer dealing with the same person who first sought medical aid. Whether it's a pain game or depression or arthritis, the suffering can still be overwhelming. Professional football players, like Joe Namath (the fabulous N.Y. Jets quarterback) often play in nearly constant pain—but how many people can stand even a hundredth of that much pain?

To protect you or someone you love, let me describe the development of a chronic pain problem so you can stop it in time. A pain appears and the person is miserable for one, two, three days. He goes to the doctor. "What is it, Doc? It's killing me!"

The physician believes he must *do* something—that's what he's been trained to do and so he goes to work. First an analgesic to relieve the pain, while he proceeds to examine, to probe and poke and test and X-ray, seeking a physical cause. Perhaps there's a hospital workup as well. In the chronic pain patient the tests will reveal nothing to account for the degree of pain—although there may be some minor spinal arthritis, some discs may show slight changes. There is never really enough to account for the severity of the reported suffering.

Meanwhile, the patient discovers that the pain is accomplishing certain things. Perhaps his teenagers behave, his children are less demanding, his mate is more attentive and solicitous, less is expected of him around the house, he can stay home from an unpleasant job. There might be accident or health insurance involved. The doctor, too—at first—is concerned and solicitous, giving his full attention to the problem.

But now the physician begins to feel his competence challenged. As the usual conventional medicine fails here (and it always does) he prescribes stronger medication. Some weeks pass— and if the time stretches into months, there isn't much hope for help from conventional medical care, although no one involved fully realizes this yet. The pain in the back (most common) or the arm, head, leg, chest fails to respond to even the powerful narcotics which the doctor sooner or later prescribes in desperation.

At some point the doctor may tell his patient the pain is functional, psychosomatic. Perhaps he even recommends psychotherapy. But the patient is resistant: "What's the matter, Doc? You trying to say it's all in my head?" The doctor is now feeling inadequate anyhow. He's got seriously sick patients and resents both taking time from them and his failure with the pain problem. So he feels hostile toward this patient who refuses to get better. This is the pain game in full force now as the patient makes a career of his pain (without being consciously aware of this). In desperation, the physician now suggests surgery—and, if you recall my views on surgery, you will see how quickly this patient is likely to find himself undergoing useless and unnecessary surgery.

Disc surgery is more often done to cut off the unending complaints than to correct any pathology. Of the 50,000 or so Americans who undergo this surgery every year, at least 20 percent (and I suspect many more) are either unimproved or get worse. Thus doctor and patient join together in the pain game, unknowing but tragic accomplices.

This country is struggling currently with a virtual epidemic of chronic back pain, to a large extent because of the unique amount of back surgery being done in the United States. My neurosurgical colleagues in Europe ask me, "Why have you got all those back pain patients?" They can't understand our problems. They don't see all this pain—partly because they don't operate on the back as much as American surgeons do.

No other land comes anywhere near our own in the number of chronic pain patients, in the percentage of devastating back problems, or in the amount of back surgery. The reason is simple: other peoples tend to accept pain and live with it; they don't demand or expect instant complete total relief from all discomfort or pain. And this is one of the major points I make in my pain clinic: "If it hurts—so what?" Having some pain is part of life. You can't expect to live without any—and if it causes no damage you're much better off if you go on functioning, learning to handle or control the pain in some simple nondrug and nonsurgical manner.

Physicians and our whole American society tend to forget what can be done. Sigmund Freud, one of the greatest medical geniuses of the last century, suffered with cancer of the mouth for seventeen years. Yet he refused analgesics because he found that they dulled his mind, kept him from treating his patients as he wanted to, and interfered with writing his papers and books. Until a few weeks before his death he fought against the cancer without drugs—and asked for the analgesics only when the end was near. Clearly pain isn't as overwhelming as Americans seem to consider it.

But the proverbial ounce of prevention is always better than a pound of cure. I urge physicians never to use drugs for pain for more than a month. If the pain persists beyond this time, both physician and patient should ask, "What should we do now?" For if it hasn't been possible to lick that pain in the first month, the doctor hasn't cured the underlying medical problem. He should stop the drugs and turn to alternative methods—to occult medicine—or he will create a complex long-lasting chronic pain problem out of a simple temporary acute one.

I see the worst pain, acute as well as chronic—the kind no one else wants to get involved with, or has already failed at. Yet, even with acute back pain I prefer wherever possible only a single day of bed rest. Two weeks in bed can make you stiff and cause your muscles to hurt just from inactivity. Extended bed rest also introduces a risk of inflamed veins and blood clots traveling to the lungs or heart. I believe in managing acute pain in a manner I call "conservatively aggressive"—and nine out of ten patients respond beautifully. The only ones who don't are those few who really do have ruptured discs—and even then I operate *only* if I can't relieve the pain conservatively. I've operated on only four ruptured discs in two years—and I have seen nearly 1,000 bad backs in this same time.

Harry had classic acute low back pain. Suddenly he couldn't straighten up. He was doubled over with excruciating pain, there was a cold sweat on his forehead, and he couldn't walk. He had to be half-carried, half-pulled into my office.

The standard treatment is still to get the sufferer into bed, apply heat to his back, keep him in bed for a couple of weeks, and use narcotics such as codeine. If there's no relief in a few days or a week, the sufferer would likely find himself in a hospital bed under traction, a sort of modern form of the old torture rack used by the Inquisition. The danger is that disc surgery may be performed unnecessarily, creating a chronic pain patient. He spends weeks in bed, and then he may be warned to "take it easy, now."

But I treated Harry the way I've found most successful. He was in bed just one day—and then he was really worked over. Ice was rubbed over the painful area: A cup of water was frozen around a wooden stick (an ice Popsicle really!) and wheeled across the painful area. Then the TNS, a simple electrical stimulator, was applied. This consists of two pads (each half the size of a deck of cards) which are taped to the back where it hurts. These pads are electrodes connected to a control box and to a transmitter about the size of a cigarette pack which controls the amount of electricity that flows through the affected area until the patient gets some relief. This was repeated as often as Harry hurt.

On the second day, Harry was out of bed with at least four ice rubs and the TNS whenever he hurt. Since there was no relief by the end of the second day, I gave Harry a vigorous acupuncture treatment at the traditional Chinese points. I used solid fine needles (32 gauge and about an inch long) and twirled them about a full turn a half-dozen times in each direction: it's a quick thing.

But low back pain is only one of the many chronic pains which yield to acupuncture. For I have had consistent successes in eliminating the pain of tennis elbow and wry neck with this ancient Chinese tool. I've even tried it in sufficient other varieties of acute pain to suggest it may have few limitations where simple acute pain is concerned—such things as tension headaches, muscle strains or sprains or aches and the like. As I've pointed out, the needles do hurt (or they won't work)—but they do no damage beyond sometimes causing a small bruise. The Chinese don't use the word "hurt" but describe it as a "sour" sensation, so this painfulness has been ignored. As you put the needle into the patient, you feel the resistance of the skin over the acupuncture points so you can almost recognize them by the slight firmness you encounter and then you press a little harder.

There is some tenderness here and I think this is probably how the acupuncture points were first located. If you hit the right spot the patient gets some numbness or heat or tingling, often feels a pain some three feet away from the point of the needle. I believe acupuncture works on pain because the acupuncture points are near major neurological pathways. I think the needles in some way affect the central nervous system through these pathways and thus relieve the pain.

With the acupuncture treatment, Harry gave a sudden sigh and said, "Oh that feels good." Within twenty-four hours he was comfortable—and started on special exercises. The combination of ice, TNS, and exercises was continued and he was discharged within a week. I find that four out of five patients with acute low-back conditions respond to acupuncture and that nine out of ten can be relieved with the whole regime. However, if there's no relief within a month or two and the patient is still in agony, he is the rare one with a ruptured disc. But even here I'll still try for three months or so (unless real neurological symptoms appear) and only then consider disc surgery. As I've said, I've only had to do this in four patients in the last two years.

My goal is the *prevention* of chronic pain problems—and this is more important than anything else because chronic pain takes an irretrievable price in agony, torment, emotional damage, personality, financial loss, and wasted life. It was through the chronic pain problem that I found this new approach to acute pain, and the TNS itself. So let's backtrack and see how it began.

In 1967, I saw Jack (whom I mentioned earlier), a man in his mid-fifties who had been virtually confined to bed for seven years since disc surgery and the resulting pain (beyond the help of narcotics). I turned to the dorsal column stimulator (DCS). I cut a hole the size of a quarter in Jack's spine and gently slipped in a carefully trimmed bit of plastic holding tiny electrodes. Then I carried wires from the electrodes along under the skin to a receiver the size of a man's wristwatch below the rib cage on a line with Jack's arm.

Jack tapes a doughnut-shaped plastic antenna to his skin, over the buried receiver. The antenna is connected to a battery-powered control box and to a transmitter about the size of a pack of cigarettes which Jack adjusts until pain is controlled. Since that operation some six years ago, Jack has been leading an almost normal life. He even reroofed his house several years ago—and all without drugs.

Bruce, an East Coast patient, injured a spinal disc during judo practice. The condition worsened and Bruce became more and more incapacitated despite four operations. "It was downhill all the way." Drugs couldn't control the pain. After Bruce had been an invalid four years, a New England surgeon inserted a DCS. Bruce could for the first time reduce his drugs sharply and start doing some work once more, for the pain is now at last bearable.

Some say that the sensation of the DCS is like a cat purring against one's arm or like the electrical vibrators barbers use to relax their customers. But I wanted to test this sensation for my-self, since an occasional patient found it too disturbing to live with. I discovered in the Midwest an elderly couple who still worked two afternoons a week making battery-operated electrical stimulators originally devised by a Naturopath some fifty years ago. This device proved useful for showing the patients what the DCS would feel like.

But I noticed that the device seemed to relieve pain on its own! So I worked with electrical engineers to build a modern elec-tronic device—the TNS or transcutaneous nerve stimulator—to control pain from the surface of the skin without the need for any surgery. It worked. There are now sixteen versions on the market, so successful has it been. It is simple and safe when used properly.

It stops acute pain more than three-quarters of the time. I've tried it on more than 1,000 people, and fewer than five in 100 find its strange buzzing vibration unpleasant. The sort of help it gives was shown when I came home one evening to find my wife stretched out on the sofa. She'd been kicked in the ankle by one of our horses. I put on the TNS and after two hours she was up and around, needed no further help or drugs, and could go about her business normally. I've seen it relieve the pain of tension head-aches, pulled muscles, and broken bones.

Neurosurgeons all over the country have reported on the TNS. In Florida, a man with a spinal cord injury was taking a half-dozen daily doses of one of our stronger narcotics trying to control his pain but he wears the TNS constantly now (even when asleep) and doesn't take drugs anymore. In Pennsylvania an aged man with lung cancer used the device and gave up narcotics.

I think the most exciting aspect of the TNS is that it is so simple and safe that I can supply patients with one to use at home. Perhaps one day it will take the place of aspirin in the ordinary medicine chest.

But the true chronic pain patient does not so readily find his way out of the tragic medical quicksand in which he is trapped. He's made pain his career and he can neither win nor get out of the game by himself. Only the new pain clinics offer a way out.

Up to the mid-sixties, pain clinics were just a collection of the usual traditional medical specialties dealing with pain conventionally—destructive surgery (cutting or destroying nerves), injections of anesthetics or alcohol, drugs.

There were no new advances in dealing with the chronic pain patient until a clinical psychologist, Dr. Wilbert E. Fordyce at the University of Washington in Seattle, turned to a thoroughly unconventional technique—operant conditioning. Only then was a way finally found to actually help these sufferers.

Operant conditioning is the way we all learn: when we do what is desired (by parents or by society) we are rewarded (candy or love or attention or a better job) and our "good" behavior is reenforced and strengthened; when what we do is disliked we are punished (reproof, silence, disapproval). Fordyce first had the pain patient checked to be certain there was no physical disability or disorder which could either cause the amount of pain reported or be worsened by activity. Then when Fordyce's patient talked of his pain, refused to function (lay down, refused to walk the amount prescribed or perform the ordered activities) he was ignored, no one spoke to him. But when he carried out his instructions—not mentioning his pain, being active as planned—he was complimented by nurses and by staff, made much of, and treated with warmth and affection. It worked—most of these pain patients recovered and began to function normally.

It seemed to me that adding physical measures to operant conditioning could speed recovery. These people do have pain but they must simply learn to ignore it when it does no damage, and activity will help the pain.

A man in his sixties was wheeled into my office with a generalized osteoarthritis (the most common kind). He had long been limited to bed or sofa or wheelchair. Using the TNS whenever and wherever he hurt, within four days he was riding our stationary bike and within a week was out walking the halls. Just the loosening up of his muscles from exercise relieved some of his pain. The activity lubricated the joints, stretched scar tissue, increased circulation. He'll always have arthritis and pain, but there'll be less of it and he'll learn to move about and live a life of increasing activity. Sure, it's not perfect—but he has help and hope here and some spice in life where there was only hopeless invalidism before.

I started my pain clinic as part of a hospital (as did Dr. Fordyce). First there's a careful neurological and physical examination which very rarely reveals any undiscovered physical reason for the pain but does determine the activity plans and how drugs will be discontinued. As I've said, almost all these patients are addicted. I have them off medication within a week or so (if their dosage is unusually high, we get them off within twelve days), simply by converting them to other drugs and then weaning them *without their knowing it*. Then I explain: "See, you didn't really need the medicine because what you're taking now is simply sugar water" (or pills or whatever I use for the particular patient).

The original hospital program took about six weeks. The patient was started with the TNS immediately and could use it as often as desired (about a quarter of them get good help promptly). I used acupuncture, too, and about a quarter responded ("Gee, that was good!") after the first treatment. A typical day started at 7 A.M. with a twenty-minute exercise period followed by a block or two of walking and then breakfast. Then I lectured for an hour on ways of thinking about pain—on biofeedback and autogenics—and then came a half hour of autogenic training to teach control of pain. Once you're in a steady alpha state you can't feel pain, as I've said. The TNS was used up to eighteen hours a day. Following the training, there was the stationary bike, the whirlpool bath and, after lunch, exercises in the swimming pool. Then occupational therapy and finally more exercises to teach patients how to go into the alpha state. We've already discussed the expansion technique and feeling for the heartbeat in the autogenic training which puts patients into deep, deep alpha states, leaving them completely relaxed.

Actually the patients were kept busy from 7 A.M. to 7:30 P.M. or later. There were ice rubs, slapping, knuckle massages, rubdowns by a masseur, and whirlpool baths. The patients were continuously moving at paces set individually for each one.

One Midwestern woman in her fifties was referred to me for a DCS since she'd had two unsuccessful disc operations. I persuaded her to try autogenics; after three months she left with her pain under control—and without surgery. A man in his mid-forties had a curvature of the spine, worsening with time, but the regular use of the TNS did the trick for him. Another who'd fallen off a ten-foot platform and suffered a herniated disc in her neck, had already had a DCS which had failed to help and she refused to try autogenics. I tried acupuncture and after the first treatment she slept through the night for the first time in five years.

Nothing works perfectly in medicine. Over 1,000 patients have been through this program in its four years and there are now some meaningful figures: 90 percent are off drugs when they leave; 80 percent have 50 to 100 percent pain relief at the end; 10 to 20 percent do backslide when they get home; and 5 percent have to be recycled, to come back for a refresher. About 10 percent quit right at the start of the program—it's too much for them. I'm looking forward to seeing the figures of other pain clinics of this type when they have had enough patients to provide meaningful statistics.

One valuable technique I've added in the past year or so has been giving the patients an opportunity to consult with Henry Rucker. More than half take advantage of it. He gives lectures regularly on ways people can think—how they can get to love themselves (because he feels most pain patients simply don't love themselves enough). Psychiatrists, incidentally, say that depression is often a matter of self-anger and we know that many chronic pain patients suffer from depression. There are also consultations, where Henry Rucker can explore problems which patients don't feel comfortable discussing with me or their minister.

One of the most valuable roles I think a psychic can fill is that of consultant because they really are superb psychologists and pick up patients' problems by clairvoyance, probing quickly and helping the patients with what are often deep-seated problems which they can't express. Henry told one patient he was still fighting his sense of inferiority to his father. With this understanding, a serious emotional difficulty was cleared out of the way so we could relieve the medical difficulties. The interviews are confidential and Henry will only warn me when there is a major problem—suicidal intent for example—which I should know for the patient's own safety and welfare.

The pain clinic is no panacea. We have to keep improving it, and this will occur as each doctor modifies the concept in his or her own hospital or center. One patient told a nurse as he left, "Boy, I can't wait to get home and back to my drugs again." We found a drug supply hidden in the false-bottom case of another. When I reproached him, he replied, "Doc, I didn't come here to get off drugs, only to cut down on my habit—it was just getting too expensive." I still wonder if this attitude mightn't have been picked up in advance by a good psychic—a new idea I hope to explore more fully later.

I am now testing out a modification of my setup. Originally I kept patients hospitalized for six weeks. Then I tried the program on a three-week schedule and found it just as successful. Then I experimented with a high-pressure twelve-day program and it still seemed to work well. Now I'm testing an out-patient plan which is simpler and less expensive for patients. The program is just like the original except for the amount of time the patient spends. As results show up, changes will be made to incorporate the best findings we have. All that really matters to me is what works best for my patients.

I see two hopeful signs in the chronic pain picture in the United States. More doctors are interested in becoming dolorologists and have been studying my clinic in order to set up their own, or just to learn how to handle chronic pain problems better. I also see, while lecturing and teaching across the country, that younger physicians are open to occult medicine and to anything else that works even if it doesn't fit in with traditional medicine. More doctors are using psychics. Some physicians are even abandoning the practice of medicine to become psychics themselves.

14

The Way of the Future: Psychic Diagnosis, Auras, Kirlian Photography, Biorhythm, the Holistic Health and Healing Centers

The specialist told the young woman she had a tumor. A hysterectomy was planned. Before the surgery, she decided to go to Olga Worrall for help. The healer said later, "When I put my hands on her I saw a baby and I thought, 'My God, this woman is five months pregnant!' " But to the woman, Olga Worrall merely said, "Before you have that operation go to another doctor and then to a third." The new doctor confirmed the healer's diagnosis—the young woman was five months pregnant.

In his book, *The Occult Explosion*, Nat Freedland reports that he took a vacation photo of himself and his wife taken three years before and placed it face-down before a famous psychic who told him that Mrs. Freedland had had appendicitis then and had seen a doctor for it. In fact, three months after the photo was taken Mrs. Freedland had had an appendectomy.

Susy Smith tells, in her book *How to Develop Your ESP*, of an English nurse whose psychic diagnostic ability has been saving lives at the Bath Child Guidance Clinic. One time the nurse begged a surgeon to take the plaster cast off a young man's broken leg. Since there was no discomfort, pain, or fever, the doctor did nothing. The nurse became virtually hysterical, imploring the doctor to take off that cast. The surgeon—just to satisfy and quiet the woman—finally removed the cast—and found a fast-spreading and deadly gas gangrene which would have cost the young man his life had it not been found in time.

This same British nurse gets odd vibrations from the tips of her fingers up to her elbows when she touches the surface of the body over a diseased or disordered organ or tissue—and so discovers medical conditions which the doctors have missed.

Sheila Ostrander and Lynn Schroeder in their 1970 book tell of a Moscow woman psychic who diagnoses diseases and of a healer in the Siberian city of Tomsk who could tell that a fully clothed man had had an appendectomy, identify the sex of the last person to look into a mirror, wave his hands over a covered photo or over eggs and then tell the sex of the person in the photo or the unhatched chicks. In Bulgaria there is the blind oracle who is famous throughout not only Bulgaria but the whole region for her ability to predict the future, locate people who have vanished, solve crimes—and diagnose diseases. This wise woman is said to be the first government-supported seeress of modern times.

How do they do it? They're really not sure themselves. Henry Rucker says, "Sometimes you get a picture, for example, of this guy's heart and you see something up there on the left side and the top." The mid-nineteenth-century "Seer of Poughkeepsie," Andrew Jackson Davis, who inspired the organization of spiritualism, claimed that he went into trances in which the bodies of human beings became transparent to him so that he could see what was going on and diagnose their diseases.

Olga Worrall is particularly skilled in psychic diagnosis—even by telephone. One family called her on the telephone about their youngster who was in pain. Their doctor had said it was only a virus but Olga said, "Virus my eye! That kid has appendicitis! You'd better get another doctor!" With another doctor and a surgeon, the child was operated on in the nick of time, for the appendix was about to burst. Olga's even diagnosed diseases in animals; she told a woman that her poodle's paralysis was due to foreign objects in its stomach and advised pumping it out. The dog recovered fully even though the vet had recommended euthanasia.

Pressed about how she is able to make her diagnoses, Olga Worrall said, "I don't know how it happens. I just know—in that precise moment, all of a sudden I know." In one case she saw clairvoyantly that a man's heart was enlarged and was certain his problem had been misdiagnosed by doctors. She urged X-rays and these showed she was right. The man got the proper treatment once the condition had been correctly identified.

No explanation fits into the framework of the sciences as we know them today. There is no way of measuring or checking for this strange talent for psychic diagnosis. All we really can say about it at this time is that it *is* there—and I will shortly go into the proof of its existence and accuracy. Data from various investigators and people who are interested confirms my own computerized study which proves in scientific terms and figures that psychic diagnosis is valid, that psychic diagnosticians are virtually as accurate as doctors with all their X-rays and devices and laboratory tests—but it still doesn't tell why. So let's first look at how these psychics make their diagnoses.

First of course is simple clairvoyance (did I say simple?) which permits those like Henry Rucker, Olga Worrall, or the others to look inside a person to see—as many psychics put it—as on a TV screen in their heads, images of the heart or other organ, the growing infant in the uterus and the like. This is not telepathy.

A deeply disturbed and concerned woman came up to see Olga Worrall before one of Olga's services at her New Life Clinic. The woman's husband was very sick and the doctor couldn't diagnose the problem. Olga somehow "knew" that he had a gall bladder disease. More doctors were called in, and made more examinations and X-rays and decided that the man had cancer of another organ, and that his life "wasn't worth a nickel." Olga continued to insist that the doctors were wrong and at the wife's urging one of the doctors spoke with Olga. An operation was performed. The other organ was perfectly normal. But the surgeon, remembering Olga's insistence, made a second incision to explore the gall bladder and there was the trouble—a large gallstone.

Many psychics diagnose by studying the "aura"—another of the mysteries of occult medicine. Many observers believe it's the visual manifestation of the energy field (love-energy perhaps?) of the human being. Some would say it's a manifestation of *Yin* and *Yang,* the energies in whose ratio lies health or disease. Whatever its source, the aura is a colorful sheath around the human being, described by psychics for centuries. It's a sort of glowing, pulsating envelope which coats the person. Psychics see it differently, though they usually agree that they see it "in the mind's eye," through their special senses and not their physical eyes.

Most agree that the aura is three-layered: tight against the skin is a sort of dark layer (some see it as blue or transparent like empty space) a quarter inch or an eighth inch thick; next is a more complicated layer, two to four inches thick and of a blue-gray color which shimmers like heat on a summer highway; and finally there is the fuzzy layer, perhaps light blue, which can be up to several feet thick. Healthy people have bright-colored auras. Disease darkens the aura.

It's possible to learn to see these auras—and, increasingly, physicians are trying to do so. One way is to gaze past the person toward a pale-colored or white wall. Another way is to look at yourself in a mirror, focusing your eyes above and behind your image. In general, the trick is to focus your eyes on something distant and see the person only as a vague outline with a rim or halo of colored light. I can personally testify that it's possible, for I'm increasingly able to see this aura around people. Where there's disease, I tend to see a sort of muddy brown color. I was able to ask a friend of mine, "What did you do to your right elbow?" and startle the living daylights out of him. "How did you know? I hurt it playing tennis yesterday!" Actually, I've always seen the energy field but I'm increasingly aware of color variations.

I strongly suspect that the really fine diagnosticians in our medical profession actually fall back on their psychic powers— "sixth sense"—to make their brilliant and startling diagnoses.

Once you're willing to approach events with an open and receptive mind, you will see some strange things, as I have, and then you have to fit them into the world as you've been taught to know it. So the question that nagged at me was "How can we put psychic diagnostic ability to real medical use?" It was important to know their rate of success, because if they were accurate in only one diagnosis in 1,000 or even 100 they wouldn't be of much value medically—only as a curiosity. I needed scientific proof of how dependably psychics can diagnose medical conditions by their own techniques.

With this in mind, in January of 1973 I brought Henry Rucker and seven of his associates at his Psychic Research Foundation of Chicago out to my clinic in La Crosse. Their job was to diagnose the problems of seventeen patients by occult means. They could see the patients face to face, have a handwriting sample and a palmprint, and know the birth date. But they couldn't question the patients.

In the initial trial the psychics really surprised me—for they proved 80 percent accurate! Physicians don't do any better than this. Clearly, psychics could be depended on to a considerable extent if further checking in greater depth were to show that the 80 percent figure held up. With a psychic whose diagnoses were accurate as often as a doctor's, the physician could obtain valuable backup information and if the psychic and the conventional medical diagnoses were the same the likelihood of accuracy would then be much greater than the 80 percent of either one alone. In short, if one missed the diagnosis, the odds are that the other would hit it.

My own psychic friends, that January in my clinic, told me

that what I feared was leukemia in one patient was actually only a liver condition—and time proved them right.

Let me share with you my thinking and the way I went about proving whether psychics really can diagnose medical conditions with sufficient regularity to make their contributions useful medical tools. I had to eliminate the possibility of lucky guesses by choosing certain specific and clear-cut cases, and enough of them to be significant.

My statisticians assured me that the seventy-eight patients whose questionnaires were to be filled out by the psychics constituted a dependable sample; this is how the Harris and the Gallup and similar scientific polls work. In short, if we took 1,000 or 100,000 patients the results should not be materially different percentagewise. So we set the number of tests to be run with this information in hand.

I chose pain patients because their problems lend themselves well to statistical analysis. It was simple to verify the location of pain. It was also more practical to limit the causes of pain to a few than to offer the psychics the whole range of all the diseases known to man and ask them to differentiate between medical conditions which even the most highly trained specialists often have trouble with. Evaluating an unlimited range of medical diagnoses would also be subject to confusion and inaccuracy.

I asked the psychics questions in three areas: the patient's personality, where the pain actually was (I provided a simple line drawing of a person marked off into twelve areas on the front of the body and ten on the back), and the cause of the pain—cancer, amputation, arthritis, scar, infection, stroke, spinal cord problems, and so on (some fourteen, all told).

It became obvious that the psychological questions required subjective interpretation, for there really is no way to measure in numbers a person's sexual adjustment, his passivity or aggressiveness, the degree of his conflicts with others, and so on. I finally decided these questions were just not objective enough for my purposes and eliminated them. I was really interested in medical and physical diagnoses which would help the average practicing physician in his or her everyday approach to a patient's medical problems.

What kinds of psychics were involved in these tests? I wanted to see how good at diagnosis a clairvoyant would be as compared to a graphologist or a numerologist or a palmist or an astrologer. I included three clairvoyants, and for my chance sample did both random sampling and asked a professor of psychology with no clairvoyant abilities to look at a photo of the patient along with his name and birth date (as the psychics did) and then fill in the same questionnaire.

To make matters more difficult for the psychics—and to eliminate the possibility that they might get some clues from the way the patients walked or moved or acted—I permitted *no* direct contacts. The clairvoyants were handed a photo on the back of which my assistant had written the patient's name and birth date. The astrologer got only the name and birth date—as did the numerologist. The palmist received a palm print. The graphologist was given a page of the patient's handwriting. The results, I feel, are filled with hope for the future.

In locating the site of the pain, the professor of psychology hit 5 percent right. But two of the clairvoyants were 75 percent accurate while the third was 70 percent correct. With the other psychics however there was a marked falloff in accuracy: the numerologist hit 60 percent right, the astrologer 35 percent, and the palmist and graphologist 25 percent. Pure chance would be 25 percent accurate—like the palmist and graphologist. The clairvoyants' 75 percent was three times what you would expect by chance, a highly significant statistical fact. In short, the clairvoyants really have something to offer diagnostically. Olga Worrall, one of the best psychic diagnosticians, is a clairvoyant. I would guess that doctors are only about 80 percent accurate in their diagnoses—not appreciably better than the psychics.

In determining the cause of the pain, the professor of psychology was a bare 10 percent accurate. The clairvoyants hit 65 and 60 percent, with the others again trailing off, from 50 percent down to 30. Once more the clairvoyants were nearly three times as accurate as chance, a highly significant finding.

In my original tests, which showed 80 percent accuracy, the psychics had the chance to see the patients. This clearly aided in diagnosis, as one would naturally expect. The fact that clairvoyants working strictly from photos were 75 percent accurate is convincing proof to me of the gift for psychic diagnosis, and also of clairvoyance, telepathy, and psychometry (for elements of all three would seem to be involved).

But scientific proof of any experiment demands replication—other investigators must get the same results. And I was very pleased to learn that this has been done.

In Central California, a psychiatrist who needs help with unusually difficult cases turns to a former internist in Northern California, who has taken up a new specialty—occult medicine. This ex-internist asks only the name, age, and location of the patient. With just this information, he can give a detailed psychiatric or physical diagnosis or both. He has achieved 90 percent accuracy with some fifty patients of the psychiatrist. This is very close to my own figures. In my initial trials, when Henry Rucker's psychics did their combined psychological diagnoses in their own way, meeting but not talking to the patients, I found some 98 percent accuracy.

Incidentally, I've used this same California internist-clairvoyant myself for personality diagnoses of some twenty-five patients and found him about 96 percent accurate. My own feeling is that the physicians who consistently make accurate diagnoses of difficult medical or psychiatric problems are themselves psychics, probably clairvoyants, even though they either don't know it or prefer to conceal the fact for fear of being looked down upon by their colleagues.

Dolores Krieger, Ph.D, R.N., an associate professor of nursing education at New York University, is 80 percent accurate at psychic diagnosis, and like so many psychics has healing powers as well. Dr. Krieger has given the name "therapeutic touch" to laying-on-of-hands. As she points out, nurses have really been doing this ever since their profession began.

While Dr. Krieger was studying the effects of a well-known healer's hand on patients, she found that the blood hemoglobin was elevated. This change occurred in one patient within forty-five minutes and it's not unusual for it to occur after a few hours. In a few patients the change lasted for several months. There has been no systematic followup because the study was intended only to provide proof that *something* happens with the laying-on-of-hands by a healer. Dr. Krieger's study was careful and extensive—and she has replicated it. She began in 1971 with a pilot study. In 1972, she studied nearly fifty subjects and thirty-three controls in depth, and an even larger number the year after that.

Susy Smith, in *Confessions of a Psychic*, reports that as early as 1956 two Soviet scientists demonstrated that white blood cell count could rise sharply when "positive emotions" were suggested, and drop when "negative emotions" were suggested. Since white blood cells are the body's chief defense against infection, these findings hold a use for—as well as a possible explanation of—faith healing.

Recently at a Council Grove Conference, sponsored by the Research Department of the Menninger Foundation, some participants presented a demonstration which took many of the physicians by surprise. Patients were brought in from outlying hospitals and a panel of five doctors had access to the medical records and findings and were permitted any examinations they themselves wished to conduct. Then psychics—one of them was Dr. Dolores Krieger—were called in to diagnose the patients. The psychics merely looked at the patients from a distance or passed their hands over the body without touching at any time. One of the medical observers—a first-rate scientist—told us that the psychic diagnosticians were 80 to 90 percent accurate in their diagnoses. He said about the demonstration, "I've certainly seen some things that have been very impressive. . . . I don't know how they could have made the diagnoses they did." Like the rest of us, he failed to understand this strange power some human beings have in greater measure than others. Only *I* want to harness it and use it in an organized way to help the sick patient. I'm convinced beyond the shadow of a doubt about the validity of clairvoyant diagnosis. However, I don't suggest that we depend on it completely. We don't know enough about it, and psychics can't offer therapy in every area so the physician should still—as always—come first.

To me there is an important lesson for medicine here—we should set up a system in which we can utilize the ability of these psychics to diagnose because if we add that to the orthodox setup, we could likely reach nearly 100 percent accuracy in diagnosis.

Let us now look at two interesting occult phenomena that may have a direct bearing on medical care but which are still in a confused gray area that we don't understand too well.

Only a few years ago, a new kind of photography came to America. Coming off the image in the photograph are flaring, shimmering, ghostly colors ranging from near-black violets to the palest blue-whites, and every imaginable shade of pink and rose and red, in lines and ridges and strange streamers. In black and white, they look like the streamers of blazing white light haloing the moon during an eclipse of the sun. This is Kirlian (pronounced "Keer-lee-an") photography—and it may tell when you're going to come down with the flu even though there are no symptoms, or when a plant is sick even though there are no apparent changes.

It all began in 1939 when (as *Psychic Discoveries Behind the Iron Curtain* tells it) a Russian electrician named Semyon Davidovich Kirlian noticed that a tiny sparkle appeared in an electrotherapy machine between the electrode and the patient's skin. Wanting to photograph the sparkle, he put a photographic plate and his hand between the electrodes and switched on the machine. He got two things—a severe burn and a photo which showed weird streamers of light coming from his fingers.

For three decades he and his wife and others in the Soviet scientific establishment have been working with what began then.

Basically it's a matter of photographing the living fireworks that are displayed when living tissues—a human finger or a leaf, say—are placed in a high-frequency electrical field. Kirlian soon discovered that he could tell whether a plant was diseased—long before the plant became visibly ill. Then one day his own photograph was hopelessly blurred and he thought the device was broken. He soon became ill and was confined to bed. His wife took a photo of herself and the device worked fine; Kirlian's photo had revealed his *coming* vascular illness. Since then, evidence has accumulated showing that the pictures are affected by nervous excitement, vodka, sickness, emotions, tiredness, or whatever.

Americans first learned of all this with the publication in 1970 of *Psychic Discoveries Behind the Iron Curtain*—and now our interest is fully aroused. It's been estimated that as many as fifty researchers in the United States alone are today working with Kirlian photography. Some of their results have been startling—and debatable.

First off, we don't really know what it is being photographed. In the basic device, a fingertip, say, is placed on the emulsion side of photographic film (color is the most dramatic), finger and film are placed between two round metal electrodes in a dark room, the current is turned on, and, finally, the film is developed. What this shows is not really known. Some think it's just an electrical phenomenon (a "corona discharge") while others see it as the body aura we've already discussed or the mystical "bioplasma body" (the "aura" of yoga literature).

The Kirlian aura varies with different people and with the same person at different times. It seems to change with emotions and physical conditions. A certain type of red blotching seems to occur only in people about to come down with the flu. Some have found differences in psychotic patients and even at different stages of psychosis. The fingertip corona of a faith healer is different before and after a healing—and so is that of the healed person.

How useful a tool Kirlian photography will prove to be is something only time and scientific research will tell. My own thought is that it might provide a way of testing numbers of people for psychic abilities and thus finding the naturally fine healers who have never recognized their powers. We may even become able to eliminate the quacks and retain only those who are really good.

There is also a new study called "biorhythm" which may also be worth considering. According to some reports, Japanese bus and taxi services were able to cut traffic accidents by 50 percent in the first year during which this system was used. The drivers were warned of their "bad" days so that they could be extra careful. It's been said that the transit system of Zurich, Switzerland, has used this system for many years, that a number of European airlines are following it, and that it's even begun to catch on in the United States. I myself have found that some 80 percent of the accidents to a group of fifty-two of my patients occurred on a critical or a double-critical day even though such days only occur 20 percent of the time. Five out of seven deaths of patients I've known in the past couple of years were also on critical days.

All you need for biorhythm is the exact date of your birth and with the proper charts and pocket calculators you can plot your own rhythm. You can also buy a Swiss watch which will give you all three cycles so that you need only look at it to know where your biorhythm is at any particular moment.

Biorhythm is based on three cycles, as explained by George S. Thommen in his book, *Is This Your Day?* First there's the twenty-three-day physical cycle of physical strength and energy. Then there's the twenty-eight-day sensitivity cycle of emotions and the nervous system. And, finally, there's the thirty-three-day intellectual cycle of intelligence and mental capacities.

The curves go up and down across the zero line on the charts supplied for this purpose. When the curves are above this line and in the positive area of the chart, they're in high gear. When they cross the zero line and drop down into the negative area they're rebuilding and recharging. The "critical" days are those when one of the three cycles crosses the zero line, either up or down. The intellectual curve isn't too important but when the others cross the zero line, watch out—for that day can be a bad one. If two curves cross the zero line on the same day that's a "double-critical" day and twice as dangerous.

My own feeling is that physicians particularly should be aware of their own critical days and should then avoid serious decisions or actions. Surgeons, for example, should not perform operations on critical days. Patients, too, should be protected by not having any surgery or potentially dangerous tests or procedures performed on them during these days. Just another way of using occult medicine to protect yourself.

Here are the steps I think the medical profession should take to provide better and more complete medical care.

I think the entire medical profession should reorganize itself to take advantage of occult medicine—just as it underwent a total refashioning when the concept that germs cause disease and infections was finally accepted only a little over 100 years ago. Medical practice was reformed from the ground up: medical school curricula were radically changed, new sciences and specialties (bacteriology for example) suddenly appeared, patient care was revamped, doctors' offices and hospitals were transformed, surgery underwent a total metamorphosis, and nursing was revolutionized.

Now I feel the medical schools should offer courses in astrology and the other occult sciences at least to familiarize the young doctors-to-be with these tools. Then medical students should be acquainted with competent psychics, to learn about clairvoyance, telepathy, and parapsychology—all the psi phenomena. They should be encouraged to develop their own psychic powers through lectures and workshops by some of our finest faith healers. It would be good for medical students to participate in healing conferences where they can see the laying-on-of-hands and what it can do and where they could talk with physicians and surgeons who are using occult medicine.

Other occult skills must also be taught the students, either as electives or required courses with actual clinical experience. In this category I would include biofeedback, autogenics, acupuncture, the electronic devices which relieve pain, and most important of all, the management of chronic pain and psychosomatic disorders. There could also be lectures and demonstrations of such new techniques and methods as biorhythm and Kirlian photography.

How can the doctor or the patient know whether a psychic is competent and honest? There is a good deal of quackery in this field; any field which has no set rules and no formal academic training or accreditation naturally lends itself to frauds. After all, you find frauds in medicine, law, accounting, and all the other professions which do have strict licensing procedures, and you will no doubt always find them wherever there are human beings.

Perhaps we might learn something from England, where faith healers are much more widely recognized and accepted, even by the medical profession itself. I myself, along with a dozen internationally recognized physicians and scientists, delivered the May Lectures, on psychoenergetics and the frontiers of medicine. I learned some interesting things. As I understand it, there is a National Federation of Spiritual Healers (NFSH) with nearly 5,000 full-time healer-members who have satisfied the requirements to be accepted. They must, for example, have been practicing healers for a considerable time and must supply the names and addresses of at least six patients whom they've treated and helped. The NFSH is simply a professional organization which tries to raise the level of practice of its members (they provide courses for further study in the field) and help them obtain recognition as healers. NFSH members are said to be able to make calls on patients in more than 1,000 national hospitals if the patients' physicians give permission; there would seem to be a good deal of cooperation from the traditional medical and paramedical professions. The president of the NFSH is the internationally famous Harry Edwards whose mail, I have been told, runs in the neighborhood of half a million letters a year.

I personally feel that there will have to be some form of accreditation for faith healers and psychic diagnosticians, either licensing or certification. It must be a formal thing, as it is today for X-ray or medical laboratory technicians, pharmacists, and nurses. I would like to see *regular training* of psychics as physician's assistants (they might be CPPAs if you will—Certified Psychic Physician's Assistants). They should be taught anatomy and physiology to increase their accuracy. In this way both the public and the level of medical care would be protected.

I'm excited by a concept I've had for some time and have been propounding in presentations to doctors across the country. It is clearly taking hold, because I've been getting calls lately to speak to groups of physicians to give advice and ideas on putting this concept into practice. First, an explanation of the key word here: "holistic" is an adjective denoting the total human being, the whole person, which includes of necessity body, mind, and spirit.

My concept—my vision maybe—is of holistic health and healing centers headed by physicians. Here the patient would find the full array of the usual medical and paramedical specialists—and also psychic diagnosticians and faith healers whom the patient's doctor can call upon in any of the many situations we've detailed in this book. This openness would bring many sufferers back to proper medical help and gradually wipe out the cultism and quackery rampant in all aspects of medical care today.

As increasing numbers of patients seek occult medicine, they would find it available as part of the total ongoing medical system—but they would be protected. The physician would be there to apply whatever conventional medical knowledge is available. The patient wouldn't find himself with conventional medical care which doesn't help enough, or have no physician to continue his ongoing care while he seeks the help of a faith healer or an additional psychic diagnosis.

In short, the holistic health and healing centers would provide a continuum of medical care which could carry the sufferer through any possible medical problem. Acupuncture, autogenics, biofeedback, biorhythm, Kirlian photography, and all the other occult techniques we've talked about would be there to be used under the umbrella of conventional medical know-how. What's more, psychics would be available for counseling should the patients desire it. Psychics might well be used for orientation lectures which might lead the patients into more regular health practices than most people have today. After all, health maintenance is much more desirable than disease treatment. Others will have ideas and thoughts that I've missed, and bring them to the centers.

I've lectured in Florida and on the West Coast and through the Midwest to doctors who are getting ready to set up their own versions of these holistic centers. We've spoken to others doing the same in New York City and there are still more we know of in Westchester County, New York, in New England, and the South.

It's clearly the way of the future—and I join you in welcoming the future with the joy and hope which accompany our new Age of Aquarius.

Selected Readings

"Acupuncture in America." *Medical World News.* July 19, 1974.

Andrews, E. J. "Moon Talk." *Journal of the Florida Medical Association.* May 1960.

Angoff, A. *The Psychic Force.* New York: G.P. Putnam, 1970.

"Biofeedback in Action." *Medical World News.* March 9, 1973.

Bonica, J. J. "Therapeutic Acupuncture in the People's Republic of China." *Journal of the American Medical Association.* June 17, 1974.

———. "Acupuncture Anesthesia in the People's Republic of China." *Journal of the American Medical Association.* September 2, 1974.

Birk, L., ed. *Biofeedback.* New York: Grune & Stratton, 1974.

Brodie, D. C. *Drug Utilization.* Dept. of Health, Education and Welfare, 1970.

Bross, I. D. J. and N. Natarajan. "Leukemia from Low-Level Radiation." *New England Journal of Medicine.* July 20, 1972.

Brown, R. F., et al. "Appraising Medical X-ray Protection Activities." *Practical Radiology,* April 1973.

Bunker, J. P. "Surgical Manpower." *The New England Journal of Medicine.* January 15, 1970.

Camp, J. *Magic, Myth and Medicine.* New York: Taplinger, 1974.

Carkhuff, R. R. and C. B. Truax. "Training in Counseling and Psychotherapy." *Journal of Consulting Psychology*. Vol. 29, No. 4, 1965.

"The Devil and Gilles de la Tourette." *Journal of the American Medical Association*. April 29, 1974.

Frank, J. D. "Psychotherapy." *American Journal of Psychiatry*. March 1974.

————. *Persuasion and Healing*. Baltimore: Johns Hopkins Press, 1973.

Friedman, H. J. "Patient-Expectancy and Symptom Reduction." *Archives of General Psychiatry*. January 1963.

Freud, Sigmund. "Dreams and the Occult" in *New Introductory Lectures on Psychoanalysis*. London: Hogarth Press, 1934.

Freedland, Nat. *The Occult Explosion*. New York: G.P. Putnam, 1972.

Hammond, Sally. *We Are All Healers*. New York: Harper & Row, 1973.

Hays, H. R. "Strong Medicine." *Physician's World*. May 1974.

Imboden, J. B., et al. "Convalescence from Influenza." *Archives of Internal Medicine*. September 1961.

Kaufman, M. R., et al. "Psychiatric Findings in Admissions to a Medical Service." *Journal of the Mount Sinai Hospital*, N.Y. 26:160. 1959.

Kunin, C. M., et al. "Use of Antibiotics." *Annals of Internal Medicine*. October 1973.

Kuhlman, Kathryn. *Nothing Is Impossible with God*. New York: Prentice-Hall, 1974.

Lambert, A. and D. Bower. "The Strange Tides that Move the Earth We Live On. *Geos*, spring 1974.

LeShan, L. *The Medium, the Mystic and the Physicist*. New York: Viking Press, 1974.

Lieber, A. L. and C. R. Sherin. "Homicides and the Lunar Cycle." *American Journal of Psychiatry*. July 1972.

Lipowski, Z. J. "Review of Consultation Psychiatry and Psychosomatic Medicine." *Psychosomatic Medicine*. Vol. XXIX, Nos. 2 and 3, 1967.

Lewis, C. E. "Variations in the Incidence of Surgery." *New England Journal of Medicine*. October 16, 1969.

Margulis, A. R. "The Lessons of Radiobiology." *Americal Journal of Roentgenology, Radium Therapy and Nuclear Medicine*. April 1973.

McClenahan, J. L. "Wasted X-rays." *Radiology*. August 1970.

Mason, R. C., et al. "Acceptance and Healing." *Journal of Religion and Health*. 8:123. 1969.

Moses, L. E. and F. Mosteller. "Institutional Differences in Postoperative Death Rates." *Journal of the American Medical Association*. February 12, 1968.

Ostrander, S. and L. Schroeder. *Psychic Discoveries behind the Iron Curtain.* New York: Prentice-Hall, 1970.

———. *Handbook of Psi Discoveries.* New York: G.P. Putnam, 1974.

"Psychic Surgery." *Journal of the American Medical Association.* 228:278. April 15, 1974.

"Reassessment of Surgical Specialty Training in the United States." *Archives of Surgery.* June 1972.

Rhine, J. B., ed. *Progress in Parapsychology.* Durham, N.C.: Parapsychology Press, 1973.

Sargant, W. *The Mind Possessed.* New York: Lippincott, 1974.

Small, S. M. and P. F. Regan. "An Evaluation of Evaluations." *American Journal of Psychiatry.* January 1974.

Smith, Susy. *Confessions of a Psychic.* New York: Macmillan, 1971.

———. *How to Develop Your ESP.* New York: G.P. Putnam, 1972.

Stewart, R. B. and L. E. Cluff. "Studies on the Epidemiology of Adverse Drug Reactions. *The Johns Hopkins Medical Journal.* December 1971.

Torrey, E. F. *The Mind Game.* New York: Emerson Hall, 1972.

Trussell, R. *The Quantity, Quality and Costs of Medical and Hospital Care Secured by a Sample of Teamster Families in the New York Area.* New York: Columbia University School of Public Health and Administrative Medicine, 1961.

Ullman, M., S. Krippner, and A. Vaughan. *Dream Telepathy.* New York: Macmillan, 1973.

Venzmer, G. *5000 Years of Medicine.* New York: Taplinger, 1972.

Webb, J. *The Occult Underground.* LaSalle, Ill.: Open Court Publishing Co., 1974.

Worrall, A. A. and O. N. Worrall. *The Gift of Healing.* New York: Harper & Row, 1965.

Index